8.95

746.4 McKain, Sharon
MCK
        The Great Noank
        Quilt Factory

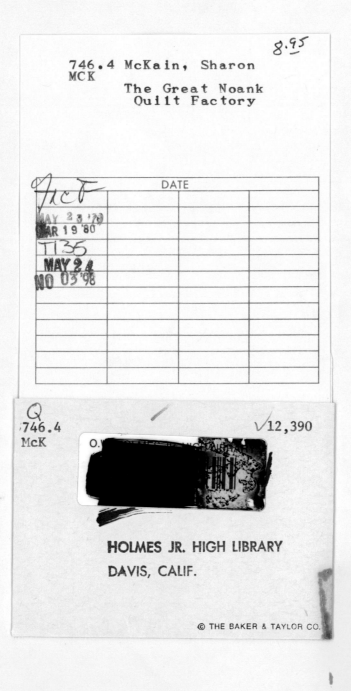

	DATE		
MAY 23 '79			
MAR 19 '80			
T135			
MAY 2 4			
NO 03 '98			

THE GREAT NOANK QUILT FACTORY

THE GREAT NOANK QUILT FACTORY

How To Make Quilts & Quilted Things

By SHARON McKAIN

Photography by HOWARD PARK
Illustrations by RICHARD M. BROWN

RANDOM HOUSE / PEQUOT PRESS   NEW YORK

Library of Congress Cataloging in Publication Data

McKain, Sharon.
    The Great Noank Quilt Factory.

    1. Quilting—Patterns.   I. Title.
TT835.M28   746.4′6   73-20568
ISBN 0-394-49064-9

Manufactured in the United States of America
First Printing

I would like dearly to dedicate this book to my grandmother, Ida Margaret Long, who with *much* loving patience taught me to sew a straight seam at the age of six.

&

to Sophie Julia Alexander, my mother, who gave me soft pieces of velvet and smooth satin to feel, and who brought from market voluptuous, purple eggplants and perfectly formed stringbeans for my delight.

I would like to thank all the people who have helped me morally, physically, aesthetically, financially, graciously, spontaneously, instructively, and joyfully on warm days, rainy days, humid afternoons and long, tired nights, with a stitch, a scissors, a scrap of calico or flannel, an idea, a hand, a book, a quilt, much hard work, and many home-favors.

Linda Alexander
Dick Baker
Laurie Brown
Richard M. Brown
Fran Capobianco
Arthur Cohen
Elaine Cohen
Tamar Cohen
Bob Craft
Patrick Cullen
Mr. & Mrs. Louis E. Fischer
Ann Fuller
Ann Glen
Bruce Glen
Peter Good
Priscilla Green
Emily Harvey
Jane Holdsworth

Howard Jonas
Ginny Jones
Jessica Jones
Lois Jones
Stephen Jones
Herta Joslin
Jane Keener
Saundra McGuire
David McKain
Joshua McKain
Megan McKain
Nancy McKain
Jean Napier
Catherine Niering
Ruth S. Palmer
Howard Park
Rieta Park

Nikki Phillips
Blanca Renado
William Ridenhour
Arlene Scully
James Scully
Unade Seckerson
Karen Steever
John Sutphen
Julie Sutphen
Sydney Van Zandt
Nancy Vogel
Dr. & Mrs. Edmund West
Roger Wilkenfeld
Zara Wilkenfeld
Bob Wilkerson
Diane Wilson
Rose York

Contents

Introduction

I don't know where or when I first saw a quilt. I may have been wrapped in one as a child or seen a picture of one in a forgotten storybook. I only know that by the age of seven or eight I had a vague idea that a quilt was warm, soft, colorful, snuggily, and made by somebody's mother. By the age of twenty my concept of "quilt" had narrowed to mean only the traditional American patchwork shapes pieced together by Early Americans and proudly displayed on grandmother's guest room bed.

Traditionally, a quilt is made of three layers—a top, a bottom called the backing or lining, and a filling. The filling is placed between the quilt top and the backing, and all three layers are *quilted* together. The *quilting* is done with a simple running stitch which goes up and down through all three layers. It may be done by machine or hand. Besides holding the layers of the quilt together, quilting creates a three-dimensional, sculptural effect on fabric. The layers of a quilt may also be secured by *tying*. A needle filled with yarn is inserted through all the layers and brought back up again; the yarn is tied in a knot or a bow.

Unfortunately, this definition of a quilt leaves out several types of bedcoverings which I would call quilts. I have seen many quilts which do not fit into the "three-layer" category. There are quilts made of two layers. There are quilts made of four or more layers and not quilted; many of the lessons in this book give instructions for quilts which are not quilted. There are quilts made of gathered circles or folded squares of fabric joined together. There are quilts made up of tiny, stuffed pillows or tubes. They look like quilts; they feel like quilts. I can only imagine that as a quilting tradition was passed from generation to generation, new methods were invented for making something quilt-like, and the thing created was called a quilt.

I first started making quilts when I got married and my husband had a king-size bed. We needed a bedspread, so I started stitching a 10' × 10' reverse appliqué quilt. It took nine months to finish, and I made two other quilts and a son during that time. The quilt I made for my unborn son, Joshua, was my first attempt at patchwork. I proceeded to get the baby's quilt together by trial and error, mostly error. I stacked up a pile of orange fabric and tried to cut out twelve triangles at once; none of them were the same size when I finished carving through the twelve thicknesses of fabric. I sewed them to some other lopsided, green triangles anyway. The mistakes I made taught me to make more and better-sewn quilts. I always finished a quilt no matter how many mistakes in cutting and sewing occurred, and each new quilt was more of a lesson than the last. The more quilts I made, the more ideas I got for new ones.

Finally I moved to a small New England town and met a woman who had been quilting for years. She taught me many traditional methods of quilt-making and gave me generous advice about short cuts. She taught me how to quilt with a proper quilting stitch, and how to "lock" the thread without a knot. If you look closely at an old quilt you will find no knots showing. The quilting appears to be done with one long, continuous thread. In Lesson 1, I will teach you the trick that Ruth taught me for locking the quilting thread firmly without knotting it.

After quilting for about five years, I started teaching classes and began to meet more and more people who were interested in quilts and quilt-making. Many of my students found faster or better ways of putting a quilt top together and we learned from each other.

I decided to write this book to answer the questions my students asked, and those a beginner might have. I have written it in the same manner I teach my students. Each lesson is for a particular technique in quilt-making. Sometimes the instructions will be for a small, sample block with directions for making a pillow or other quilted items. You will always be able to make something from your sample piece. You may want to make several quilted pillows, handbags, back packs, place mats, or a wall-hanging, incorporating a few different sample blocks instead of making a large bed-sized quilt from each lesson. I will teach you the quilting technique and suggest what quilted items you can make from the sample piece you have sewn. You may, of course, think of others.

Quilting is simple and easy to learn, but in learning any new technique you may feel clumsy at first. If you have not sewn before, a needle will feel awkward in your fingers; a thimble may feel like a huge stone and seem more of a hindrance than a help to your quilting. The initial discomfort of trying something new will soon disappear. You will establish a quilting rhythm as easy as breathing. You will enjoy quilting, and have a good time.

10

The Great Noank Quilt Factory

I am the Great Noank Quilt Factory. The place where I turn out quilts has changed from time to time. When the factory started operating it took up a very small space in a very small apartment. I was short of capital at the beginning and bought fabric by the half-yard. I would sit anywhere with my quilting in my lap, and a pair of scissors, a needle, a thimble, and a spool of thread within easy reach. As the quilt I was working on grew, I enlarged the factory to include the floor around me. I got so excited about making quilts, I made more and more. They began to pile up and I gave them to friends. My friends showed these quilts to other friends, and the Wadsworth Atheneum in Hartford, Connecticut, asked me to design and make a quilt for their textile collection. I was overdelighted. They sent me a check and I bought a $50.00 sewing machine.

The factory expanded to the dining room table of a New Hampshire farm house. As my husband and I, and two children moved from apartment to apartment, the factory changed location. Large tables make good quilt factories. When we finally came to Noank and bought an old Victorian house, I used a roomy upstairs hallway where I set up my sewing machine and ironing board. Scraps of fabric and lint and thread covered the floor, and got tracked throughout the house. The quilts kept piling up and I began to sell some.

One summer, my husband, and some friends and I, insulated and wired the old boat house we used for a garage. I moved all my quilting gear out there, bought a new pair of scissors, several bolts of broadcloth and continued to quilt like a mechanical woman. As interest in quilting grew, I decided I would like to teach the craft. I gave free lessons to several neighbors and found they liked quilting and I liked teaching. This was about the time that I decided that small as the quilting operation might be, it was indeed a sort of factory — The Great Noank Quilt Factory.

The factory has now moved to another location. People have heard about a quilt factory in Noank and this summer many have stopped by to see it. They seem surprised and a bit disappointed when I take them into my living room and they see only a table with a sewing machine, my spool rack filled with thread, a couple of old chests, large shelves with books and assorted junk, my two luxurious avacado plants, and fabric, paper, pencils, and scissors strewn about the floor. They ask if I am *really* set up, if this is *really* a quilt factory. I say, "Yep, this is it!"

11

Things You Will Need

You probably have many of the things you need for quilting in your home already. If you want to set up a small factory for yourself, you will need the items listed below. When other materials or tools are needed, I will list them at the beginning of each lesson.

> scraps
> well-sharpened scissors
> thread
> #7, #8, #9 needles, "betweens" and "sharps"
> a box of straight pins
> paper
> pencils
> cardboard
> yardstick or ruler
> thimble

Scraps

You will be surprised to see how a bag full of odd scraps can become a large quilt. If you do not already have a scrap bag, just let your friends and neighbors know you need scraps, and in a week you will probably have enough fabric to make a few king-sized quilts.

Quilters take a great deal of pride in using up scraps left over from making a dress, a shirt, or another quilt. Some quilters even feel it is unlucky to make a quilt with new, *bought* material and will only use scraps. I am not suggesting that you or your friends save every little bit of material in hopes of making a quilt, but usually a large hunk or two of fabric is left over from each sewing project and the scraps pile up. Some scraps can be as large as a few yards—perhaps some fabric bought to make a dress which was never sewn. Very small scraps can also be used for many of the lessons in this book. My students delight in using the tiniest scrap, especially if it is a favorite color or print.

Scissors

I now have about five pairs of scissors. You only need one well-sharpened pair. If your scissors are in good condition they will cut smoothly through fabric without fraying it at the edges. I have one pair of scissors which I use for cutting paper and cardboard. They are old and rusty and my children are allowed to use this pair for their sewing and cutting projects. Cutting paper and cardboard will soon dull a pair of scissors and they will not cut fabric easily. I also have a pair of very small scissors which I like to use for removing basting and cutting small fabric pieces and thread while I am hand-sewing.

Thread

I use mostly heavy-weight mercerized cotton thread for sewing and quilting. Polyester thread stretches and knots if you use it for hand-sewing. Quilting thread is also available now. It is cotton thread which has been treated to make it stiff. The stiffness is supposed to prevent knotting. If your yardage shop does not carry it, ask them to order some.

Needles

Needles come in various sizes which are appropriate for different types of sewing. The higher the number of a needle, the thinner it becomes, and its length is distinguished by the words "sharps" and "betweens." The "sharps" are about 1 1/2″ long and the "betweens" are about 1 1/4″ long. "Betweens" have always been used for quilting, and needle companies are now starting to put the label "quilting" on each package of "betweens" since the current quilting revival began.

When I first started sewing, I would always buy a package of "assorted" needles and soon found that I had many needles which I never used. Unfortunately, since the package *was* assorted, I had no idea how to buy the size of my favorite needles. Now, I prefer using a long, skinny needle, a "sharp," when I sew and quilt.

For quilting or appliquéing and other hand-sewing, you will probably want to experiment with needles #7, #8, and #9, both the "sharps" and "betweens," until you find the most comfortable size for your rhythm of sewing. These needles are thin and small-eyed. Thin needles tend to bend and you will need more than one to finish a quilt. Once a needle becomes bent, throw it out. When I made my first quilt I felt a strange loyalty to my needle and sewed with the same one until I finished the entire 10′ × 10′ quilt. Struggling to sew with a bent needle can be very frustrating.

Pencils

I use a regular #2 lead pencil when I mark fabric. Occasionally, on very dark, patterned fabrics, I will use a light colored drawing pencil. I have found that tailors chalk or marking pencils make too thick a line around the outside of a cardboard pattern. Ball-point pens leave globs of ink which might smear and stain a pretty patch.

Cardboard

The best cardboard to use for making a permanent pattern is thin and strong. The cardboard that comes stuffed in laundered shirts is excellent. You could also use the cardboard boxes from breakfast cereals or crackers.

Thimble

If you have never used a thimble, go and buy one as you would try on shoes. It is worn on the index finger of your sewing hand. Try on a few sizes to see which size is comfortable for you. It should fit loosely but not fall off your finger. It is like a little, metal hat and the side of the thimble is used to push the needle through fabric. Pretend that the thimble is not on your finger and push your needle with the same part of your finger as you would normally do when sewing without a thimble. The tip of the thimble is not used, as some people might think, to hammer the needle through the fabric.

Sewing Machine

When I first started quilting, I borrowed a sewing machine from my neighbor. After using her machine off and on for a year, I bought an inexpensive one of my own. I still have that $50.00 machine and I have never felt the need for a more expensive or fancier one. You do not have to rush out and buy a new machine to start quilting, especially if you have never sewn with a machine before. Ask a friend to lend you hers for awhile and to show you how it works. It is not difficult to learn to use a sewing machine. I have taught many beginning quilters how to sew with mine, in about twenty minutes.

A sewing machine is not absolutely necessary for making quilts, but it makes your sewing a lot faster and stronger. All your quilt patches or blocks which call for a straight seam joining them, can be stitched on a sewing machine. In place of hand-quilting, you may also quilt by machine to join two or more layers. Even though some quilts are made almost entirely by hand, there are times when your sewing machine will come in handy. There are quilts in this book which may be made without any hand-sewing. The Strip Quilt in PLATE 16 was made entirely by machine and finished in a few days.

Hoop

You will not need a quilting frame or a hoop for each technique described in this book. For the traditional three-layered quilt made in a large size, either a frame or a hoop is useful when putting your quilt together. The reason for using a frame or a hoop is to keep the layers of your quilt flat and smooth as you quilt through them.

If you do not have a frame or a hoop, you may baste the layers of your quilt together to keep it smooth while you do the actual quilting. If you are planning to quilt by machine, you should always baste the layers of your quilt together first. To do this, smooth the layers on a floor—good side of the quilt backing facing down, filling smoothed over the backing, and quilt top with its good side facing up—and baste them together with *very* large running stitches radiating from the center to the edges of your quilt. The basting may be done with large, long, sloppy stitches as long as they hold the layers together smoothly while you do the smaller, neater quilting. The basting will look like large spokes radiating from the center of your quilt. You then baste concentric circles out from the center, creating a giant spider-web of basting stitches to hold the layers of your quilt firmly together. When you begin quilting, move from the center out. Remove all of your basting stitches when the entire quilt has been quilted. Some quilters baste their quilts, and use a hoop in addition.

A quilting hoop is like a very large embroidery hoop. The one I use is round and measures 22″ in diameter. *(Illustration 1.)* Some hoops are oval and come with a stand. Hoops can be purchased through mail order companies, or you can ask at the shop where you buy fabric if they could order one for you.

If you use a hoop, you begin your quilting stitches in the center of your quilt. To put the hoop on your quilt, first smooth the three layers of your quilt on a floor in their appropriate order, and slide the inside ring of the hoop carefully under all three layers right in the center of your quilt. Then, place the outside ring of the hoop on top of the quilt directly over the other ring centered underneath the layers. Gently push the top ring down and adjust the clamp on it so that it fits snugly onto the bottom ring. *(Illustration 2.)* Remember that the purpose of the hoop is to keep the three layers smooth, not to stretch them. Check the backing of your quilt which is inside the hoop to see that it has not bunched up. When you have finished quilting the area of the quilt within the hoop, remove the hoop, smooth the whole quilt on the floor once more, and fasten the hoop onto a new area adjacent to the quilting you have just finished. Keep quilting, and moving the hoop from the center out, until the entire quilt is quilted.

Frame

Quilting frames may be purchased through mail order companies, but it is often easier to make one yourself. The simplest and best frame I have used is made by tacking mattress ticking to four 1″ × 2″ boards. A useful length is 8′ for two boards and

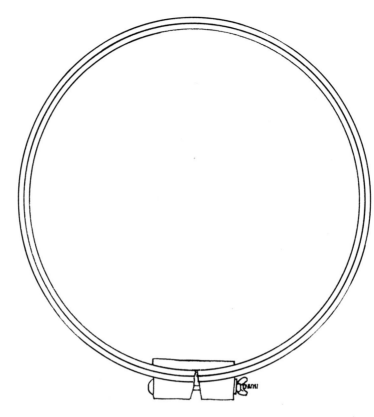

Illustration 1

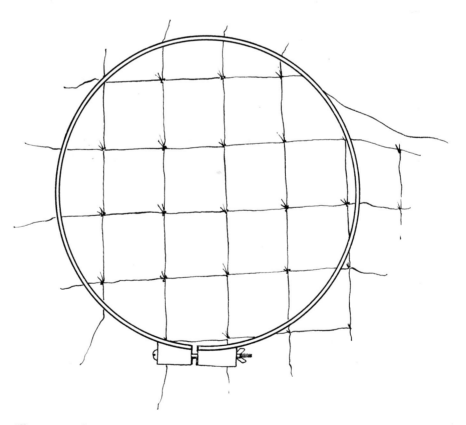

16

Illustration 2

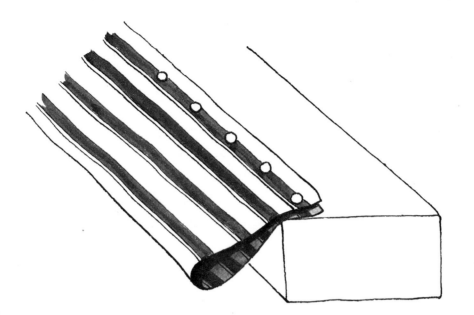

Illustration 3

7′ for the other two. The boards should be chosen carefully to be sure they are not warped. The mattress ticking is as long as the board, and about 4″ wide. It is folded in half lengthwise and tacked to the board so that it hangs over one side about 1 1/2″. The tacks are spaced about 2″ apart. *(Illustration 3.)*

You will also need four 4″ C-clamps to secure the corners of the frame when it is in use. C-clamps can be purchased at a hardware store and asked for by that name. They are called C-clamps because they are shaped like the letter C.

To put your quilt on the frame, smooth the layers of the quilt on a clean floor, and place one frame board, with the mattress ticking up and facing the quilt, along one side of the quilt. Pin through all three layers of the unfinished quilt and through the mattress ticking on the frame. Start pinning the quilt layers to the frame at the center of a frame board. Smooth the quilt layers toward the ends of the board as you pin. When you have finished pinning one side, pin the opposite side of the quilt to another frame board the same length as the board you have just done. Pin the remaining two sides of the quilt to the other two frame boards, and C-clamp the boards at the corners. *(Illustration 4.)* Remember that the purpose of the frame is to keep the quilt layers smooth, not to stretch the quilt. You are not trying to make a quilted trampoline.

When a quilt is on the frame, the frame and the quilt will fill a room. Your quilt will now be attached to its frame and lying flat on the floor with each corner firmly C-clamped. You can prop it up on a table or some chairs and begin quilting. I usually put a chair at each end of the quilt and rest the frame boards on the chair seats. I can

17

Illustration 4

then sit at the side of my quilt and begin quilting or tying. When using a frame, you quilt or tie from the edges of the quilt, toward the center. When you have quilted or tied as far as you can comfortably reach from every side of the frame, unpin the sides of two opposite ends of the quilt from the ticking, unclamp the C-clamps and roll in the ends, fastening the C-clamps in the new position. *(Illustration 5.)* When you have finished quilting or tying the entire quilt, unpin it from the frame and bind the edges with bias tape. The frame boards and C-clamps can then be stored easily.

18

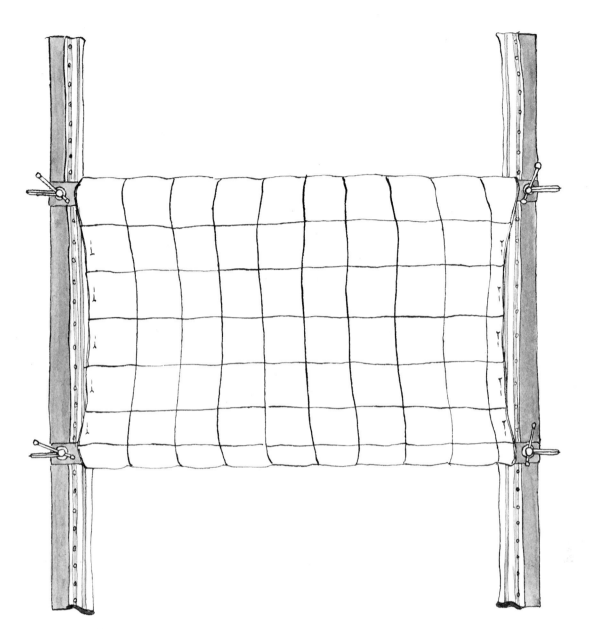

Illustration 5

EXPLANATION OF SEWING AND QUILTING TERMS AS USED AT THE GREAT NOANK QUILT FACTORY AND SOMEWHAT IN THE ORDER THEY APPEAR IN THIS BOOK

good side or
right side

When I use the words "good side" or "right side" I am referring to the surface of the fabric which would be *outside* if you made a dress. Some fabrics are "good" on both surfaces. Others have a definite "good" side on which the color or print is brighter and clearer.

straight or
grain, versus
bias

Fabric is woven on a loom. Threads are secured to the front and back of the loom in parallel rows, called the warp, and other threads, called the weft, are woven over and under these parallel warp threads thus making cloth. The "straight" or "grain" of the fabric runs with the warp threads and also, perpendicularly to them, with the weft threads. The fabric is strongest and stretches least when pulled with the "grain." The "bias" of the fabric is a diagonal line running through the warp threads at a 45° angle. *(Illustration 6.)* It is not a line that can be *seen;* it only exists as a location among the warp and weft threads. Sometimes your quilting or sewing instructions will tell you to cut, fold, or place a pattern "on the bias."

seam

A seam is made by joining two pieces of fabric by placing their two good sides together and sewing down one common edge. The "seam allowance," or size of the seam in sewing small patches together, is usually 1/8" to 1/4". That is about as

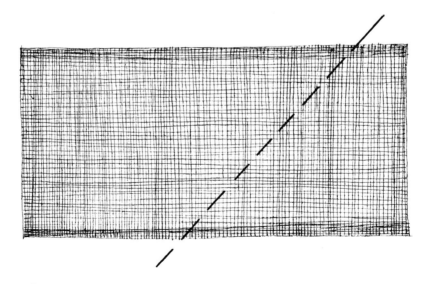

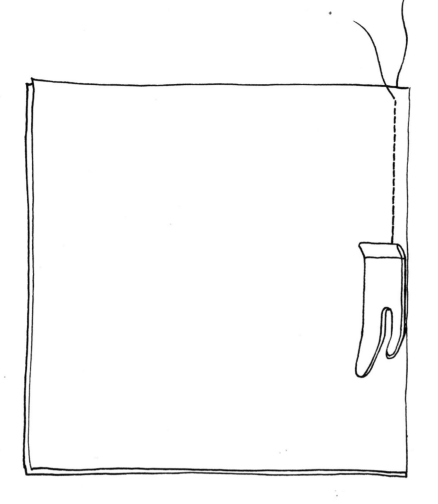

Illustration 7

small as a seam can be without fraying and coming apart. The presser foot on a sewing machine has two "toes." The smaller "toe" is about 1/8″ wide and can be used as a guide while making seams by machine. *(Illustration 7.)* There will be lessons in this book when a larger seam allowance will be given.

bias tape

Bias tape is made from strips of fabric cut on the bias and ironed with small folds along each side. It is made especially for finishing edges and can be purchased at any yardage shop. Most quilts are bound with bias tape to finish their ragged edges. A "border" on a quilt is not the binding, but part of the quilt top, and is quilted just like the rest of the quilt. After the quilt top has been quilted to a filling and a backing, the ragged edge of the three layers is bound with bias tape.

selvage	The selvage runs down both sides of a bolt of material. It measures between 1/4″ and 1″ in width depending on the fabric. It is more tightly woven because of extra warp threads which strengthen the sides of the material as it is being woven. This helps to keep the fabric even at the edges. Cotton usually has selvages about 1/4″ wide, and when I cut patches for quilt-making I use the selvage. Some selvages have printing or numbers on them, or are a very different color or texture from the material between them, and you would not want to include them in your patches.
unbleached muslin	Muslin is a fine, heavy cotton fabric which used to be inexpensive. Unbleached muslin is beige or cream in color and rough looking—a poor man's linen. It was used frequently in old American quilts. It is a strong material and useful for lining flimsier fabrics. Being the peasant of cotton, it was used frequently when a large quantity of fabric was called for. Unfortunately, it is just as expensive as other cottons today, but its strength and traditional use makes it desirable for many quilting techniques.
broadcloth	Cotton broadcloth is a smooth, fine fabric of medium weight. It used to be a common fabric for making shirts. 100% cotton broadcloth is excellent for quilt-making.
fancy fabric	The use of the word "fancy" is particularly prevalent in old quilting instructions. I find it a very descriptive word. It means *any* fabric which is colorful, whether plain or printed. When I use the term, "very fancy," I am referring to luxurious materials such as velvet, satin, velveteen, brocade or silk.
calico	I use the word "calico" as it is used in America. It is *any* printed cotton, but usually evokes a certain amount of nostalgia.
patch or piece	A patch is a small geometric shape cut from fabric. Many patches are sewn together to make a design. A quilt made up of these small geometric shapes—triangles, squares, diamonds—is called a patchwork quilt. "Piece" is another word for patch, and a patchwork quilt may be referred to as a "pieced" quilt.

22

block	A block is a section of a quilt with a complete design on it. Usually several blocks are made and sewn together to make a bed-sized quilt.
quilt top	A quilt top is the decorative, quilt-sized layer of a quilt before it is secured to the filling and the backing. Most of your sewing efforts will be in creating the quilt top whether it be in patchwork, trapunto, appliqué or another sewing technique. Many old quilt tops which never became a finished quilt, have been found in attics, chests and antique shops.
down	Down is the small, very soft feathers taken from the neck and breast of geese, ducks or chickens. You can order down by the pound from feather importing companies in large cities. If you can find a few old down pillows or comforters in someone's attic, all the better! This summer I heard of a very ambitious young woman who got her down directly from the chickens she kept. When I called another friend to ask if she knew anyone who made down quilts, she said, "No one that's alive today!"
filling	Quilts may be filled with cotton batting, dacron batting, flannel, old wool or cotton blankets, old towels, down, or even nylon stockings or sponge rubber. Dacron filling, which will be mentioned in some lessons, is a synthetic material which looks like cotton, but is lighter, fluffier, and holds together better than cotton. It comes in "bats" (long, rolled-up, wide strips usually the size of a single bed blanket). Or, you can buy it by the bag in loose pieces. It looks like white cotton candy.

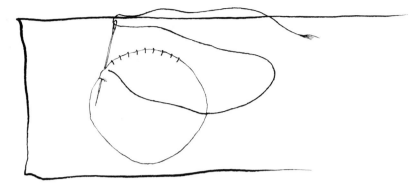

Illustration 8 Appliqué Stitch

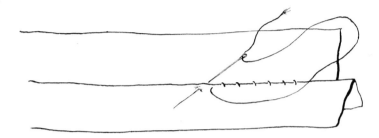

Illustration 9 Hemming Stitch

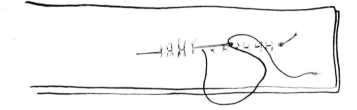

Illustration 10 Running Stitch

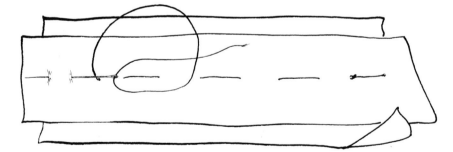

Illustration 11 Basting Stitch

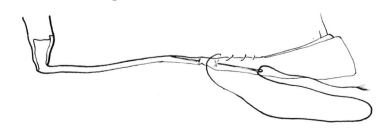

Illustration 12 Invisible Stitch

1   The Pot Holder [See PLATE 2, page 34.]

The things you learn from making your first quilt are terribly important to all the quilts following. The first lesson in this book is how to make a small quilt—a pot holder. A pot holder is the smallest quilt there is, but once you have made it, you can go on confidently to bed-sized quilts. This is perhaps the most important lesson in the book for it explains *exactly* how to put a three-layered quilt together. You will learn how to cut patches, sew, iron, quilt by hand, and bind the finished piece. For those who have sewn before, the instructions may sound over-simplified, but for those unfamiliar with needle and thread, these basic directions are quite necessary. Using this method you can make place mats, bags, and very large quilts.

This pot holder may be made with several different scraps or in the traditional nine-patch which is a checkerboard of two different colors or prints. You will need five squares of one color and four of another to make a nine-patch pot holder.

Besides the common essential items listed in *Things You Will Need*, for this lesson you will need:

> 3″ × 3″ cardboard square
> some scraps of fabric
> 9″ square of old blanket or towel for filling
> 9″ square of cotton broadcloth for backing
> 1 package of 1/2″ wide bias tape

Cutting:

If your scraps are wrinkled, iron them before you begin. Place your cardboard pattern on your fabric going with the grain (you can start right up against the selvage) and carefully outline it with a pencil. When you have drawn all nine squares (four of one color, five of another) cut them out following the pencil lines. *(Illustration 13.)* You must always draw and cut one square at a time—trying to shortcut by stacking fabric and cutting all the squares with one stroke only results in imperfect squares which will not fit neatly together into a quilt.

Sewing:

Set your patches into the nine-patch checkerboard pattern on a table exactly as they will look when finished. Take the first two patches in the top row and, with the good sides face to face, sew them together with a 1/8″ seam by machine, or by hand with a tiny running stitch. *(Illustration 14.)* Next, sew the third square in the top row to the other two. *(Illustration 15.)* Sew the patches together in the other two rows the same way. When all three rows are seamed, pin the top row to the center row (good sides facing) making sure your top seams are directly over the center row seams. *(Illustration 16.)* This insures that your squares fit together at right angles. Do not

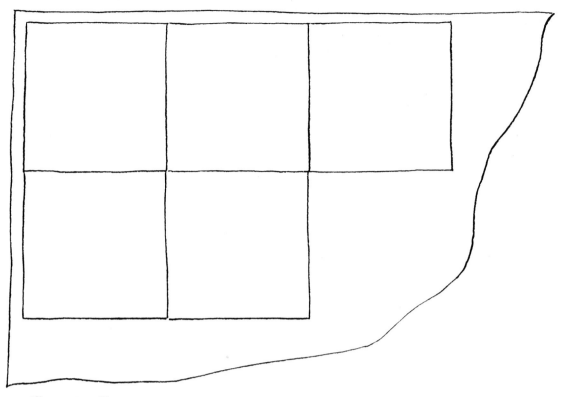

Illustration 13

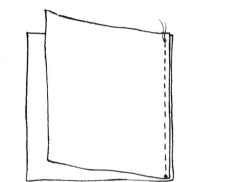

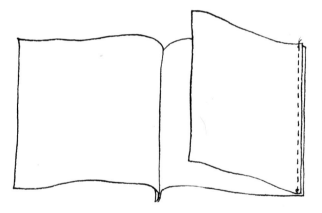

Illustration 14

Illustration 15

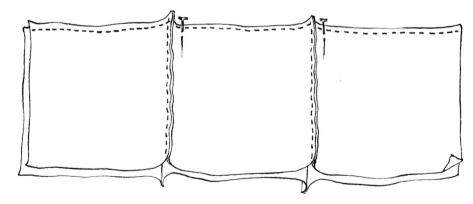

Illustration 16

Illustration 17

worry if the ends of the rows are not even, or if the material between the seams bunches a bit. It is where your seams join that effects the overall pattern. Sew the third row to the other two rows.

You have now finished your "quilt top." Iron the quilt top with the good side up. Just squash your seams flat and do not bother about which direction they lie.

Quilting:

Place your 9″ square backing on a table with the good side down, then your "filling" (the 9″ square of blanket or towel) over that. Center your quilt top (the nine patches you have sewn together) over the filling and backing with the good side up. Pin all three layers together, putting one pin in the center of each square. *(Illustration 17.)*

27

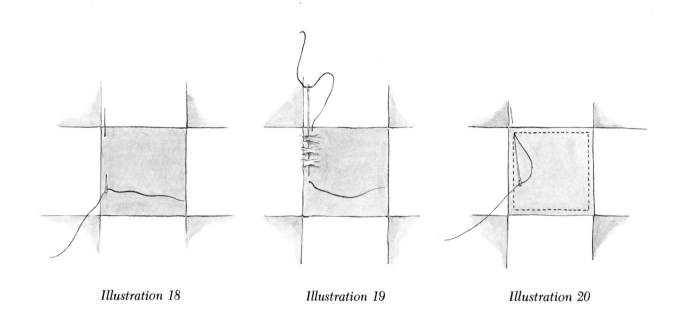

Illustration 18   *Illustration 19*   *Illustration 20*

In quilting you never knot your thread; you lock it. Thread your needle with a single thread and DO NOT knot it. (A double thread is never used for the actual quilting. Two threads rubbing together over even a short time will break sooner than a strong single thread.) Insert your needle about a needle-length away from a corner of the center square. Slip the needle between the layers of fabric and come up at the corner about 1/4″ away from the seam. At this point, the needle and thread DO NOT go through the backing, merely anywhere between the layers. *(Illustration 18.)* Leave a little "tail" where you first inserted your needle and start taking little, tiny, running stitches *through all three layers* back toward the direction of the "tail." *(Illustration 19.)* This locks the thread and is your "knot." When the thread is locked, snip off the "tail." Your stitches should be as long as they are far apart—the same length on the back as on the top.

If you have never used a thimble, start now! It may feel uncomfortable at first, but it will save you much pain if you intend to be a quilter. *(See Thimble, page 14.)* It is hard to get used to any new tool but soon it will seem to be a part of your hand.

Quilt around the center square until you are back at the corner where you began, then once again slip your needle between the layers and come up in the corner of an adjacent square 1/4″ from the seam. *(Illustration 20.)* Quilt to the edge of your pot holder and then slip the needle between the layers and come up in the next square. You do not quilt around the outside of the pot holder. *(Illustration 21.)* The outside edges of your pot holder will be secured with bias tape binding when you have finished quilting it.

You will need to thread your needle more than once to quilt the entire pot holder. When you find yourself almost out of thread, end the quilting the same way you began it—slip the needle between the layers and come back under where you have just quilted about a needle-length. This again locks your thread in place of a knot. Snip the "tail" of thread which remains when you have pulled your needle through.

28

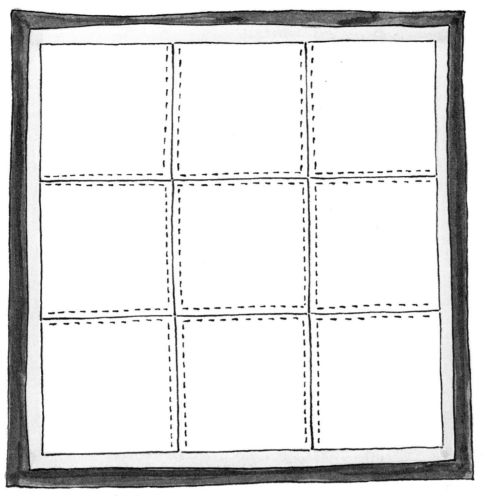

Illustration 21

Binding:

The bias tape comes pre-folded. It is 1/2″ wide with a 1/4″ folded under on each side. Unfold the bias tape and place the good side of the tape against the quilt top, and pin it around the pot holder. As you start pinning, fold about 1/2″ of the end of the bias tape back over itself and pin it down. *(Illustration 22.)* Start pinning in the center of an edge of the pot holder. Do not begin pinning on a corner or you will have a lot of tape bunched into the corner. Continue pinning around all the sides of your pot holder. Turn the corners carefully, being sure the pleat which occurs when you turn the bias tape is pinned down so that it will not get caught as you sew. *(Illustration 23.)* Now, sew with a tiny running stitch in the crease of the outside fold of the bias tape all around the pot holder. Remove your pins, and trim the excess material of the layers of the pot holder to the edge of the bias tape. Fold the tape to the back of the pot holder and hem by hand. Your first quilt is finished!

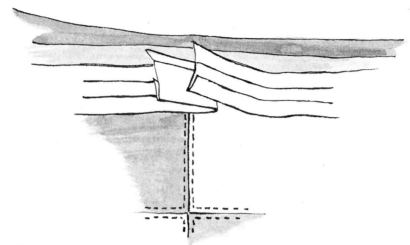

Illustration 22

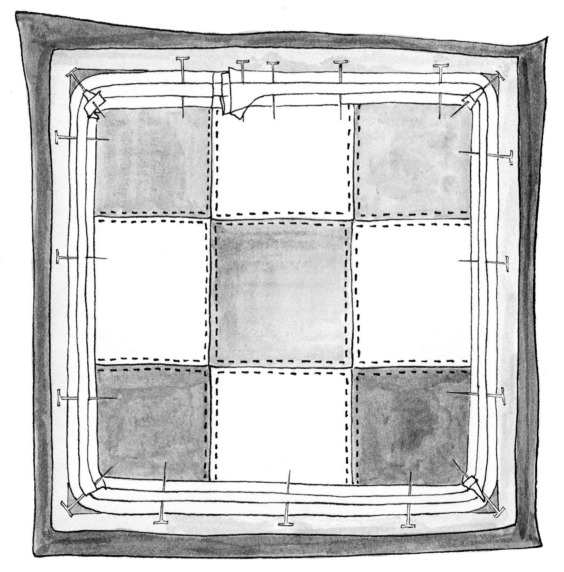

Illustration 23

2   The Tied Quilt   [See PLATE 1, page 33; PLATE 3, page 34.]

You are probably anxious to start a project more ambitious than a pot holder. After a friend of mine made her first pot holder, she was so excited about quilting that she wanted to do a large quilt immediately. This lesson will teach you the method of tying a quilt, with specific instructions for making a double-bed quilt. The quilt top is put together in the same manner as the pot holder, by sewing square patches together.

For your first large quilt you should use fabrics of similar weight. Different weights of fabric stretch and fray in different ways, and the combination of burlap and silk, for instance, might create an added difficulty as you sew. Cotton broadcloth is durable and easy to sew. It is ideal for your first large quilting project. You must also remember when choosing fabric that the quilt top will be attached to a filling and a backing, making the finished quilt very warm and heavy.

Since sewing square patches is the simplest method for making a patchwork quilt top, you will eventually want to experiment with many different fabrics using this technique. If you use heavy fabrics such as velvet, corduroy, wool, linen, denim or upholstery fabric, you may decide not to put a filling in your quilt. You would simply tie the heavy quilt top to a backing. Many layers of fabric become quite heavy; the first quilt I made was a burden to sleep under, and I would fold it away each night.

The yardage and instructions given below are for the double-bed quilt pattern in PLATE 1. You can follow this pattern or make your own quilt pattern on graph paper and then figure the yardage you will need.

For this lesson you will need:
> 5″ × 5″ cardboard square
> cotton string or yarn for tying
> a sharp, large-eyed needle
> an old blanket for filling
> 3 packages of 1″ bias tape

fabric	36″ wide	45″ wide
blue	1 2/3 yards	1 2/3 yards
yellow	2 2/3 yards	2 1/3 yards
green	3 yards	2 1/3 yards
backing	8 yards	5 yards

Cutting:

Using your 5″ × 5″ cardboard square as a pattern for your patches, draw and cut 76 blue squares, 122 green squares, 116 yellow squares, and stack them neatly next to your sewing machine, if you intend to use one. Remember to draw and cut each square individually as you did for the pot holder.

Sewing:

Allow a 1/4″ for all seams. Referring to PLATE 1 often, start sewing your first row of squares together. Reading the quilt pattern in PLATE 1 from left to right, sew the first two squares together, with the good sides facing, then the next two, etc. Then, sew the first two joined squares to the second two. Keep repeating until you have sewn all the squares in the first row to each other. (To save time and thread, sew in assembly-line fashion. Sew two patches together at a time, and then without pulling the first two patches from your machine, sew the next two, then the next two, etc. Your pairs of sewn patches will all be attached to each other by threads which can be clipped before you start sewing the pairs together.) Set the first row aside and begin sewing the squares for the second row in the same manner. When the second row is finished, pin row 1 to row 2 with the good sides facing. Be sure the seams are matched where you pin them. Pin as often as you feel is necessary. Sew the two rows together allowing a 1/4″ seam. Repeat with every two rows. Be sure to keep checking the quilt pattern in PLATE 1 as you sew. If one square or row is out of place, it will show up drastically in the finished quilt.

When you have sewn all the rows together, your quilt top is finished. Iron it on the good side, squashing the seams flat on the underside.

The Backing:

If your backing fabric is 36″ wide, cut three lengths 90″ long and sew them together along their selvages. For 45″ wide fabric, cut two lengths 90″ long and sew them together with a 1/4″ seam joining the selvages. Iron the seams in one direction. I find ironing the seams in one direction strengthens the seam and prevents it from splitting open as the quilt wears.

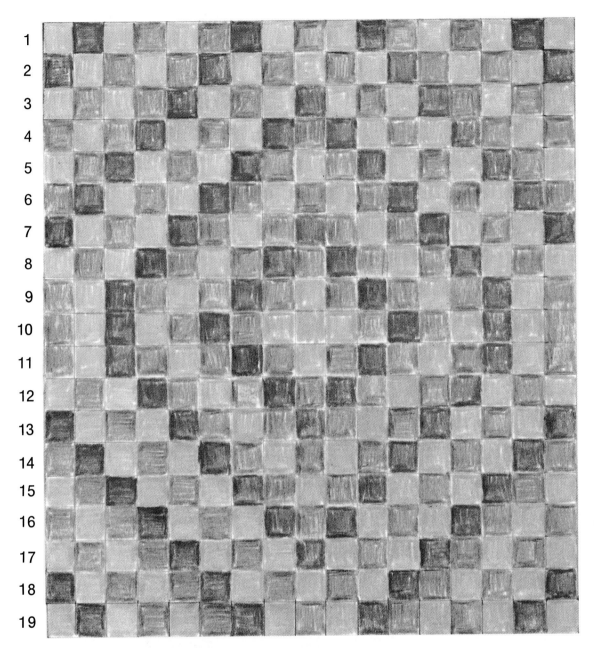

Plate 1   The Tied Quilt Pattern, Lesson 2, page 31.

PLATE 2   Nine-Patch Pot Holders, Lesson 1, page 25.

PLATE 3   Julie's Tied Quilt, Lesson 2, page 31.

34

PLATE 4   The Puff Quilt, Lesson 3, page 43.

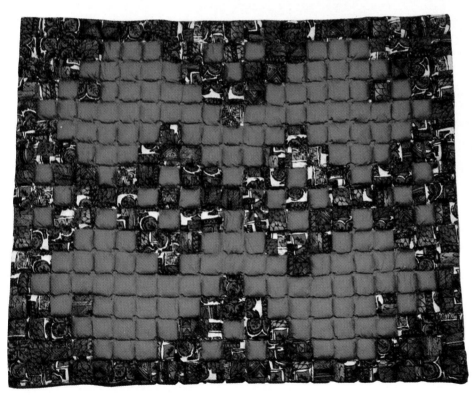

PLATE 5   The Biscuit Quilt, Lesson 4, page 45.

35

Plate 6   Rose of Sharon Quilt, Lesson 5, page 47.

36

PLATE 7   Rose Cross Quilt, Lesson 5, page 47.

PLATE 8   Joshua's Birthday Quilt, Lesson 5, page 47.

PLATE 9   Lady Bug Quilt, Lesson 5, page 47.

PLATE 10   Hawaiian Pillows: Tulip, Orchid, Pineapple; Lesson 6, page 51.

PLATE 11   Hawaiian Pillows: Shell Ginger, Plumeria; Lesson 6, page 51.

40

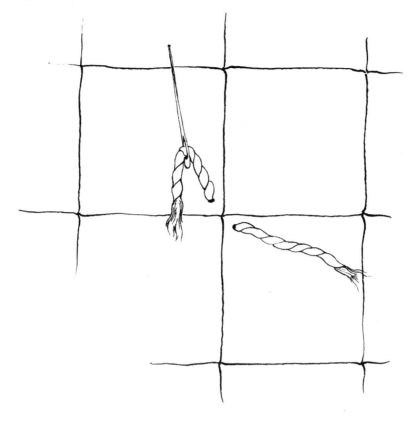

Illustration 24

Tying:

Lay the backing on a clean floor with the good side down. Center the old blanket on top of the backing. (You may have to piece two old blankets to make a filling which is as large as your quilt top.) Center the quilt top with the good side up.

A quilting frame is the best thing to use when putting a tied quilt together. A quilting hoop may be used in place of a frame. *(See Hoop and Frame, page 15.)* If you do not have a frame or a hoop, pin the quilt in every square through all three layers. You may need more than one pin per 5″ square. If you decide to pin the layers of your quilt together, begin tying in the center and smooth the layers gently outward to keep them flat as you tie.

After you have temporarily secured the three layers of your quilt by one of the above methods, you will begin tying. Thread your sharp, large-eyed needle with yarn. You may double the yarn for a fluffier "tie" but do not knot it yet. Now, tie the quilt by inserting your needle (through all three layers) 1/8″ from the corner of a diagonal square. *(Illustration 24.)* Tie a square knot and snip the ends of the yarn about 1/2″ long, or a length you prefer. You can tie the quilt from the back or on the quilt top as illustrated. When you have finished tying every corner joining each square, bind the quilt with 1″ bias tape. *(See Binding, page 29.)*

41

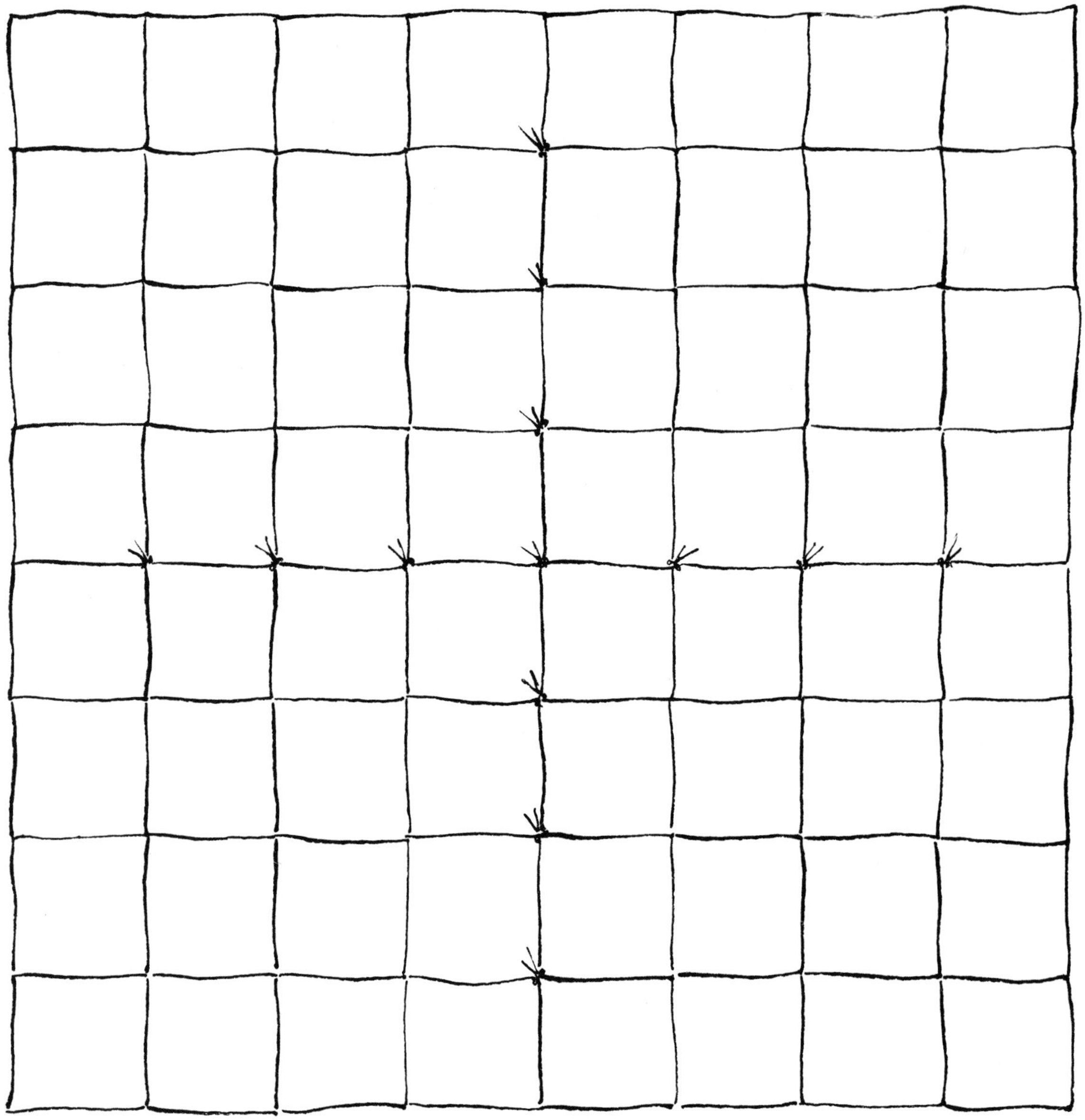

Illustration 25

42

3 The Puff Quilt [See PLATE 4, page 35.]

The Puff Quilt is composed of squares which are stuffed before they are sewn to each other. Each fancy square is sewn to a muslin backing square and stuffed with a handful of dacron fiber. Since each patch is pre-stuffed, there is no need for a blanket filling in this quilt. After all the fat, stuffed squares have been sewn together, a fancy backing is tied to the puffy quilt top to cover the ragged seams.

This lesson gives directions for a quilt which will measure approximately 45″ × 45″. It is an ideal size for a baby, newborn to one year. If you want to make a larger quilt, simply sew enough puffy squares to cover your bed, and then sew them together.

For this lesson you will need:

> 6″ × 6″ cardboard square
> 2 1/3 yards 36″ wide unbleached muslin
> 2 1/3 yards 36″ wide fancy fabric
> 2 yards of fancy fabric for backing
> 1 bag stuffing (dacron or polyester fiber)
> cotton string or yarn
> a sharp, large-eyed needle
> 2 packages of 1″ bias tape

Cutting:

Draw and cut 64 muslin squares using your cardboard pattern. Draw and cut 64 printed or colored squares from the same pattern. If you want a checkerboard effect, you will need 32 squares of one fancy fabric and 32 squares of another.

Sewing:

Place each fancy fabric square on a muslin square with the good side up. Sew the squares together around three sides with a tiny running stitch 1/4″ away from their edges. Leave the fourth side open for stuffing. When you have sewn all 64 "pockets," stuff them with a handful of dacron or polyester filling. (A rounded handful is more than adequate, over-stuffing will make it difficult to sew.) Sew up the fourth side on all your "pockets."

Now all your squares will look like miniature pillows with a ragged edge surrounding them. Sew them together in rows of eight, good sides facing, allowing 1/2″ seams. This seam will hide the stitches which joined the fancy patches to the muslin. It is difficult to sew stuffed squares to one another and you will probably have to pin them together before sewing, to keep them from popping away from each other. They will not fit easily under the presser foot of your sewing machine; you can mash them as they slide under the foot.

Pin the top row to the second row, good sides facing, with the seams matching. Continue sewing rows together until your quilt top is finished.

Tying:

Measure your finished quilt top and cut a backing two inches larger all around. You may have to piece two lengths of fabric together to get the proper size backing. Place the backing on the floor with the good side down. Center the quilt top over the backing with the good side up. Tie through both top and backing at the corners of each square as you did in the Tied Quilt. Start in the middle of the quilt and work out to form a cross, smoothing the quilt top and backing toward their edges as you tie. (*Illustration 25.*) Be careful to keep the backing and the quilt top smooth. If you have one, a quilting frame works best for tying this puffy quilt.

When you have finished tying your quilt, bind it with 1″ bias tape. (*See Binding, page 29.*)

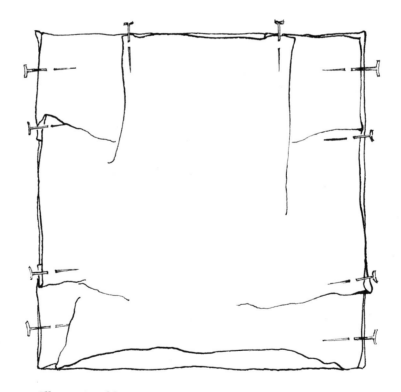

Illustration 26

44

4 The Biscuit Quilt [See PLATE 5, page 35.]

The technique for making the Biscuit Quilt is similar to the Puff Quilt. Each "biscuit" section is stuffed before they are joined to each other to make the quilt top. The only difference is that the fancy square is larger, and pleats are taken to make it fit onto the muslin square. The extra fabric in the top fancy square makes it stand up in a "biscuit" shape when stuffed.

The Biscuit makes a very plush pillow or a quilt that everyone loves to poke and touch. Some of my students have increased the sensual quality of this quilt by making the "biscuits" out of velvet or velveteen. So that you can learn quickly the method for making this quilt, I will give directions for a 16″ square pillow. If you wish to make a large quilt, simply lengthen the rows of "biscuits" until they are the desired size.

For this lesson you will need:
> 6″ × 6″ cardboard pattern
> 4 1/2″ × 4 1/2″ cardboard pattern
> some scraps of fancy fabric
> muslin
> stuffing (dacron or polyester fiber)
> 20″ square of fancy fabric for the pillow back

Cutting:

Draw and cut 16 muslin squares with the 4 1/2″ pattern. Draw and cut 16 fancy squares with the 6″ pattern.

Sewing:

With the good side up, pin the corners of the larger, fancy square to the corners of the smaller, muslin square. Then, take two pleats on one side of the larger square and pin them to the muslin. Pin pleats on three sides and sew around the pinned sides about 1/4″ from the edge. (Illustration 26.) Leave the fourth side open for stuffing.

Now, you have sixteen baggy "pockets" with ragged edges. Stuff the center with a handful of dacron or polyester filling. (Stuff very full if you are making a pillow, and just until it holds a "biscuit" shape, if you are making a quilt.) Pin the pleats on the fourth side, and sew it closed 1/4″ from the edge. You have now made sixteen "biscuits." Sew the "biscuits" together, four in a row, with the good sides facing, allowing a 1/2″ seam. As in the Puff Quilt, this seam will hide the stitches which join the fancy square to the muslin. You will have some difficulty sewing these fat, stuffed

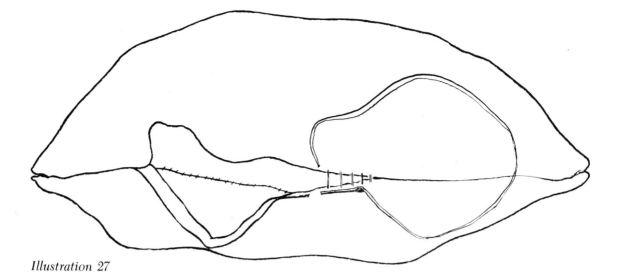

Illustration 27

"biscuit" squares together. Pin them well, to mash them flatter as you sew your seam. Then sew the rows together with the good sides facing. Your "biscuit" quilt top is finished!

To Make a Pillow:

The finished "biscuit" sample will be the front of your pillow. You will also need a back. Measure your finished quilt top and cut a back for your pillow 2″ larger than the top all around. Line the back of the pillow with muslin to strengthen it, by sewing the fancy back, good side up, to the muslin 1/2″ away from their edges. Now, measure the size of your quilt top from the stitches of one side of the quilt top to the stitches of the opposite side. Draw a square on the muslin lining of the pillow back the same size as your measured quilt top. Pin the back of the pillow to the quilt top with the *good sides facing.* Pin through the pencil line directly on the stitches around the perimeter of the quilt top. The Biscuit Quilt is so fat and puffy that it is difficult to sew the pillow back to the front evenly. The "biscuits" will push the flatter pillow back, away. That is why pinning directly on the pencil line is so important before you sew.

Sew just inside of the pencil line around 3 1/2 sides of the pillow. Leave an opening for stuffing. Turn the pillow inside out and stuff. Invisibly stitch the fourth side closed. *(Illustration 27.)* Your pillow is finished.

If you are making a large quilt, measure your finished quilt top and cut a backing 2″ larger all around. Lay the backing on the floor with the good side down. Center the quilt top over the backing with the good side up, and start tying as you did for the Puff Quilt. If you make a very large Biscuit Quilt, you should use a frame for tying. *(See Frame, page 15.)* Because the Biscuit Quilt is so puffy, a hoop does not work well for tying it. When your quilt is tied, finish the edges with bias binding. *(See Binding, page 29.)*

46

5 Appliqué [See PLATE 6, page 36; PLATE 7, page 37; PLATE 8, page 38; PLATE 9, page 39; PLATE 30, page 101.]

Appliqué is one of the oldest methods of making a fancy quilt top. The ancient Egyptians, Chinese, Indians, Europeans, Americans and Central Americans have used this traditional technique to embellish their quilts and quilted garments. It is a very satisfying way to work because any shape you can imagine can be cut out and applied to a larger piece of fabric.

An appliquéd quilt may be made up of many joined blocks with pictures appliquéd on them, with or without borders separating each block. A large, bed-sized piece of fabric may also be appliquéd with smaller shapes to create a huge picture or scene. A friend of mine recently showed me an appliquéd picture she had found in an antique shop. It was of George Washington praying in front of a campfire before crossing the Delaware. The piece was very elaborate with bare trees in the background, and many small pieces to make up Washington's clothing, boots, cape, and famous hat.

There are many, many traditional appliqué patterns which were popular in Early American times and they have lovely old names. There are several old appliqué patterns known as the *Rose of Sharon*. For this lesson I decided to make a new *Rose of Sharon* pattern in the traditional style. When you have finished this lesson you will have a sample appliquéd block measuring 20″ × 20″. You may use your sample as the center for a Medallion Quilt, for a pillow, bag, back pack, or join it with more blocks to make a large quilt top.

For this lesson you will need:
- some scraps of fabric (calico or plain colored cotton)
- 20″ × 20″ square of plain colored cotton or unbleached muslin for the background of the quilt top
- 1 package of 1/4″ bias tape for stems

Cutting:

Trace on paper and cut out the patterns for the *Rose of Sharon. (Illustration 28.)* Place the patterns on the material you have chosen and carefully draw around them. Cut exactly on the lines you have drawn. Cut as many fabric pieces from one pattern as the illustration indicates. Now, baste each piece by turning under an 1/8″ hem all around. *(Illustration 29.)* Your basting stitches need not be very neat, just close enough to hold the material under. It may be difficult to turn under and baste at

47

Illustration 28   Rose of Sharon

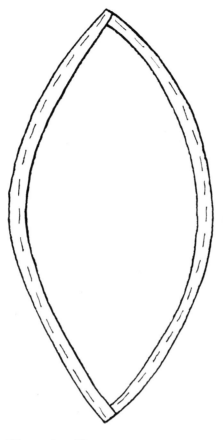

Illustration 29

points or *V's* of the pieces. Just do the best you can, and do not worry if some of the edges become a little frayed.

Sewing:

When all the pieces have been basted, arrange them on the 20″ × 20″ piece of background fabric. Do this on a smooth surface so that your material will not bunch or wrinkle while you appliqué. Now, pin all the pieces down the way you want them. (SEE PLATE 6.) Some quilters baste the pieces to be appliquéd to the background fabric. I find that pinning is faster and works just as well for traditional appliqué.

Appliqué Stitch:

The appliqué stitch is a simple overcast stitch coming up through both the background fabric and an edge of the piece to be appliquéd, and going back into the background fabric perpendicular to the edge of your pattern piece. *(Illustration 30.)* A

49

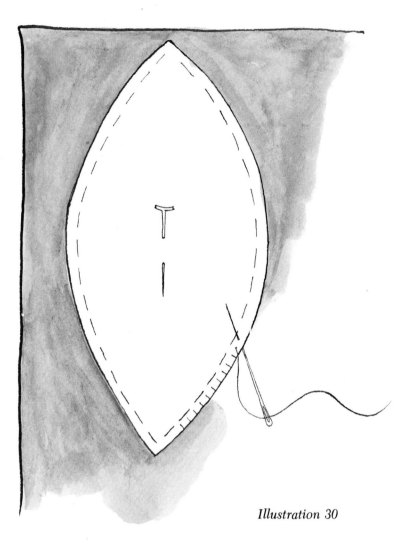

Illustration 30

double or single thread may be used. The thread is knotted and the knots appear on the underside of the background fabric.

Generally, it is best to start appliquéing from the center of your quilt top or block, out toward its edges. If you have left any wrinkles, they can be smoothed out as you appliqué.

When you have appliquéd all the pieces, carefully remove your basting stitches with a tiny pair of scissors and a pin.

6 The Hawaiian Quilt [See PLATE 10, page 40; PLATE 11, page 40; PLATE 12, page 73; PLATE 13, page 73.]

The early missionaries brought quilting to Hawaii, but the natives adapted the technique to the needs of their own culture. Their designs are taken mainly from the flora of Hawaii and, supposedly, no two are alike. Each quilter creates her own pattern and signs each quilt. The designs are carefully guarded by the quilters and it is not easy to copy one. It has been said that the patterns are created by outlining the shadow of a plant.

The method for making a Hawaiian Quilt differs only slightly from traditional appliqué. Instead of several small pieces creating a design or picture, one piece of fabric is folded and cut to make a symmetrical design. Only plain colored fabric is used in traditional Hawaiian quilting, never a gingham, calico or other printed material. The appliqué stitch is used to secure the Hawaiian design to a background, but this design is not hemmed with a basting stitch as were the tiny pieces for the *Rose of Sharon*. The ragged edge of the Hawaiian design is turned under as you appliqué.

The designs shown in *Illustrations 31, 32, 33, 34,* and *35* can be varied slightly by wandering from the pattern with a slight curve or loop when cutting. These quilts are often individualized by cutting *pukas* (slits or holes) along the bias fold.

After experimenting with this technique, you may want to make a bed-sized Hawaiian quilt. To make your own design for a quilt, get a large piece of paper. Newspaper can be taped to make a large sheet, but butcher paper or wrapping paper will make a sturdier pattern. Fold the paper according to the folding instructions, and draw a pattern. Cut it out, open it, and see what happened. Folding is the most important step in making this quilt. If it is not done carefully you could end up with several bits of fabric rather than one symmetrical piece. You may remember how you made paper snowflakes as a child, by folding a sheet of paper and cutting curves and holes along the folds. If you did it properly, when you opened the paper, you got a snowflake; if not, you got confetti.

In passing on any traditional quilting technique, I feel great respect for the individual quilters who created artfully designed patterns for themselves and others. Hawaiian quilters are fiercely proud of their designs. They take great pains to create each original pattern and are very conscious of the flowing, plant-like lines of each design. Their patterns represent, in highly stylized form, the leaves, blossom, and fruit of a particular plant. A giant *snowflake* would be considered a very poor Hawaiian pattern. These proud, old quilters would beat their students with a stick for producing a thoughtless design! You will probably want to make several experimental paper designs before you create one you like well enough to use for a bed-sized quilt.

In this lesson, I will teach you the technique for making a Hawaiian Quilt, giving instructions for a pillow-sized sample. The patterns in *Illustrations 31, 32, 33, 34,* and *35* vary in size and will create larger or smaller pillows accordingly. (See PLATE 10 and PLATE 11.)

Illustration 31 Tulip

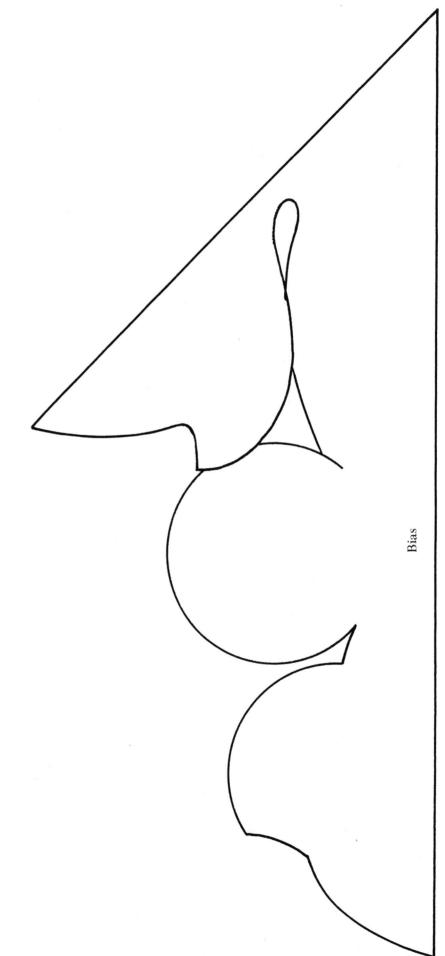

Bias

52

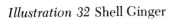

Illustration 32 Shell Ginger

Bias

53

Illustration 33 Beauty of Honolulu (Orchid)

Bias

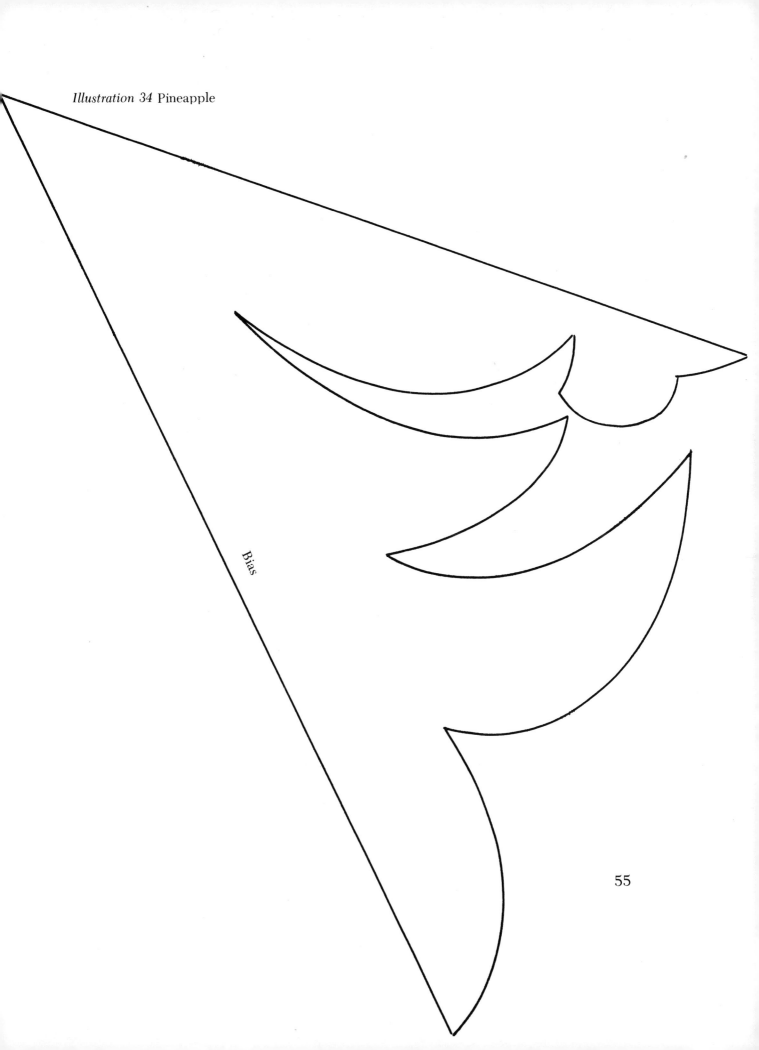

Illustration 34 Pineapple

Bias

55

Illustration 35 Plumeria

Bias

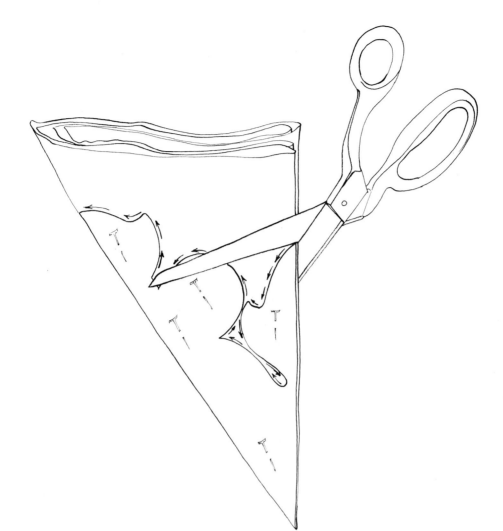

Illustration 36

For this lesson you will need:

        scissors (sharp to end of point)
        #7 needle
        thread to match both colors of fabric
        2 yards plain colored fabric (100% cotton)
        1 yard different colored fabric (100% cotton)
        1 yard cotton flannel
        2 yards unbleached muslin for backing
        (all yardage given is for 36″ wide fabric)

Illustration 37

Illustration 38

58

Illustration 39

Folding:

Iron all your material well before beginning.

Place a square yard of the solid colored material you have chosen for the symmetrical design on a flat surface. FOLD THE BOTTOM TO THE TOP AND CREASE THE FOLD BY HAND. (DO NOT IRON FOLDS.) FOLD THE LOWER RIGHT CORNER OF THE FOLDED EDGE TO THE LOWER LEFT CORNER. CREASE THE FOLD. (Now there will be one fold on the right, two folds on the bottom, and open edges on the left and top.) MAKE A TRIANGLE BY FOLDING BOTH FOLDS OF THE LOWER LEFT CORNER TO MEET THE RIGHT FOLDED EDGE. CREASE FOLD. The lower right point of the triangle thus formed is the center of the pillow and is called the *piko*, meaning middle. All folds should extend outward from it.

Cutting:

Trace on paper and cut out one of the patterns in *Illustrations 31, 32, 33, 34,* or *35.* Place your paper pattern on the folded fabric triangle with the edge marked BIAS on the bias of the fabric. *(See Bias, page 20.)*, and the point of the pattern at the "piko". Pin firmly through the pattern and all eight layers. Then cut around the pattern. *(Illustration 36.)* Do not cut through the fabric folds. If your scissors are not sharp, you will not be able to cut through all eight layers easily, and the edges of your design will be frayed.

59

Appliquéing:

Place a square yard of fabric you have chosen to be the background on a smooth surface. Center the unfolded Hawaiian appliqué piece on it. Baste the two pieces together from the center out. *(Illustration 37.)* Baste around the inside of the appliqué piece about 3/4″ from the edge.

Begin appliquéing the symmetrical design to the background from an edge near the center. (Your thread should match the color of the symmetrical piece.) As you appliqué, tuck under the raw edges about 1/8″. Your needle is a good tool for tucking the edges under. Just slip it along the raw edges, turning them under with the side of your needle. You may have trouble at the sharp curves and points, but do not snip any curves or V's, just force the edges under with the needle and take closer, smaller stitches. When the top is appliquéd, pull out the basting stitches.

Quilting:

Place the muslin backing, the flannel filling, and the Hawaiian quilt top, facing up, on a smooth surface. Baste through all three layers from the center out, to hold them together as you quilt. You should use thread which matches the color of the fabric you are quilting. Begin quilting on the background fabric, around the perimeter of the symmetrical design. This first row of quilting should be very close to the design, but definitely on the background fabric. *(Illustration 38.)* Your second row of quilting will be inside the symmetrical design, 1/2″ from its edge. Continue quilting toward the center of the design, with rows of quilting 1/2″ apart and parallel to the perimeter of the design. (Although you start quilting from the perimeter to the center, when the entire design has been quilted, the parallel rows of quilting stitches appear to be radiating from the center of the design in increasingly larger concentric shapes.) When the appliquéd design has been quilted, quilt the background with rows 1/2″ apart and parallel to the perimeter of the appliquéd design. Quilt out toward the edges of the background fabric until you have quilted this entire area. *(Illustration 39.)* Remove the basting stitches carefully.

7   The Dresden Plate [See PLATE 14, page 74.]

The Friendship Ring is another name for the Dresden Plate. When quilting bees were a part of early American life, a quilter would collect scraps from her friends and have a different piece of fabric for each "spoke." The same kind of sharing still goes on today. My friends and I sit around and talk and quilt. Everyone enjoys finding out differences and similarities in each other; the way one woman will combine fabrics and colors is very different from the way another might. We all like to see and touch the various fabrics in each other's scrap bags, and exchange pieces. Many warm memories go into a patchwork quilt. Everytime I see a certain patch, I am reminded of the person who gave it to me.

The Dresden Plate is a combination of pieced work and appliqué. Several "spoke" pieces are sewn together and then appliquéd to a plain block. It is a relatively easy block to make, and looks like a fancy, decorative plate when finished.

The Dresden Plate is also a good pattern for "block by block" quilting. Most quilts are put together in three quilt-sized layers—the quilt top, the filling, and the backing. Even quilts made up of blocks are not quilted until the blocks and borders have been sewn together to make a large quilt top. However, some quilts lend themselves easily to "block by block" quilting. Any quilt made of blocks can be put together by taking each block separately and quilting it to a filling and a backing, before the whole quilt is put together. Each block becomes a tiny three-layered quilt. This method is very useful if you are planning to quilt by machine, or if you enjoy hand-quilting a small block in your lap rather than the weight of a full quilt. You do not need a frame or a hoop for this type of quilting.

In this lesson I will teach you the technique for making *one* Dresden Plate block, and give instructions for making a single-bed Dresden Plate quilt in the "block by block" method.

For this lesson you will need:
> scraps of fabric
> 22" × 22" square of plain colored fabric for the background

Cutting:

Trace on paper, and cut out the patterns for the "spokes" and the "center" of the Dresden Plate. *(Illustration 40.)* Draw around the patterns and cut sixteen fabric spokes and one center for each Dresden Plate. You may choose to have sixteen different calicos and plains, or set up a pattern of alternating fabrics.

61

Illustration 40   Dresden Plate

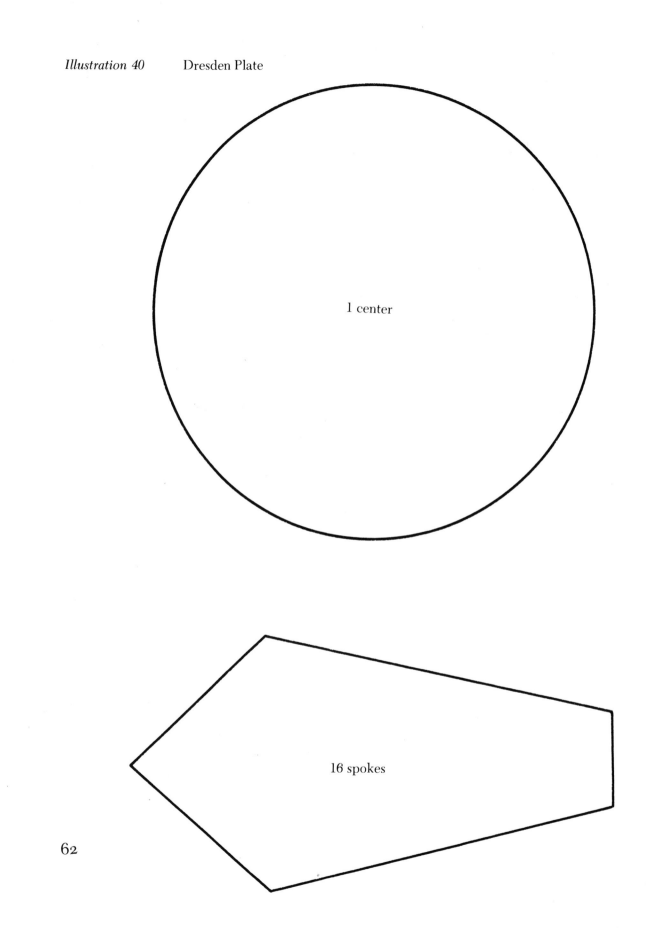

1 center

16 spokes

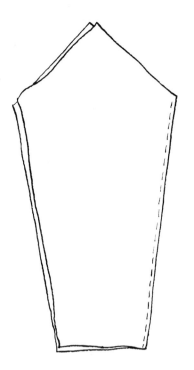

Illustration 41

Sewing:

When all your pieces are cut, sew one spoke to another spoke, by placing the two good sides together and sewing down one side. Allow a 1/8″ seam. *(Illustration 41.)* Repeat until all sixteen spokes are sewn in pairs. Then sew two spokes to two spokes, good sides facing; then four to four, and eight to eight, until you have a circle of spokes. Now, iron the circled spokes with the good side up, just squashing the under-seams flat.

Next, as in traditional appliqué, turn under a 1/8″ hem and baste around the outside of the circled spokes, *(Illustration 42.)*, and around the outside of the center circle. Now, center the circled spokes on your background block. This can easily be done by folding the 22″ × 22″ square in fourths and gently pressing with your fingers to crease it at the center. When the block is opened, you will have a cross in the middle which will make it easier to center the circled spokes. Pin the circled spokes to the block through the center of each spoke. Pin down the center circle over the hole in the circled spokes, in about four places. Be sure you have kept your material smooth while pinning.

Start appliquéing around the center circle first, and then around the outside of the spokes. When you have finished appliquéing the "plate" to the block, remove your pins and pull out your basting stitches carefully.

If you intend to make a single-bed Dresden Plate quilt in the "block by block" method, you will need to make nine Dresden Plate blocks in the above manner.

Illustration 42

Illustration 43

Block by Block Quilting

I cut the backing for each block 3″ larger than the Dresden Plate block, and the filling the same size as the Dresden Plate block. (Material gets "taken in" a bit when it is quilted.) The extra fabric in the backing blocks makes it easier to sew the quilted blocks together later. Center the filling over the backing and the Dresden Plate block on top of the filling, good side up. Pin or baste all three layers together. Quilt the block, through all three layers, around the inside of each spoke, around the inside of the center circle, and around the outside of the plate if you choose. Remove the basting or pins.

When you have quilted all nine blocks, sew them together, three blocks in a row, by placing the backing of one finished block against the backing of another, and sewing a 1/2″ seam down one side. The ragged seam will show on the top of the quilt row. You will have three rows of three blocks each. Do not sew the rows together until you have covered the raw seams in each row with borders.

Cut six border strips about 6″ wide and as long as a block. You will need two border strips for each row. Iron under a 1/2″ hem down each side of each strip. Place the strips over the seams joining the blocks in each row. Pin these strips in place, and sew down both sides of each strip, very close to the edges, and through all the layers of fabric. (*Illustration 43.*)

Illustration 44

When you have finished sewing borders to cover the ragged seams in each row, sew the rows together by placing the backing of one row over the backing of another row, and sewing a 1/2″ seam down one side. The raw seam joining the rows will show on the quilt top and can be covered with a border, just as the other raw seams were. You may cut a long 6″ wide border for this, or shorter border strips separated by 6″ squares. (SEE PLATE 14.)

When the rows have been joined and borders added to cover the raw seams, you will want to make a border for the outside edges of the quilt. (The outside border is not a binding. Bias tape is always sewn on last to finish the quilt.) The outside borders should be the same thickness as the quilted blocks, so you will be adding borders made of three layers—a top, a filling, and a backing. This can be done by first adding a long strip of backing material about 6″ wide, and as long as the quilt top, to one edge of the quilt. Place the good side of this backing strip against the backing of the quilt and sew it to the edge of the quilt with a 1/2″ seam. Fold this strip out from under the quilt. Iron the raw edges of the seam toward the outside edge of the backing strip. Then cut a strip about 6″ wide and as long as the quilt, for the top border of the quilt, and a strip of filling the same size. Place the good side of the top border strip facing the quilt top, with one edge of this strip against the stitches of the raw seam which joins the border backing to the quilt. Place the filling strip over the top border strip and sew through both strips at once and through all the layers of the quilt, allowing a 1/2″ seam. *(Illustration 44.)* Fold the top border and the filling back over the backing strip. You have now created a three-layered border for one side of your quilt.

Sew a three-layered border to the opposite side of your quilt in the same manner. Then repeat the same instructions for the top and bottom borders. You may want to sew contrasting squares to the ends of the last two top border strips to be added. Bind the three-layered borders with 1″ bias tape around their ragged edges. *(See Binding, page 29.)*

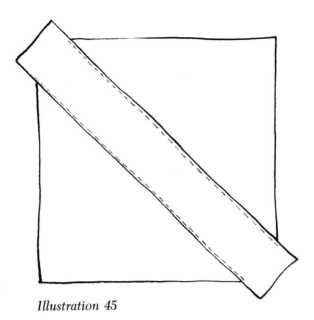

Illustration 45

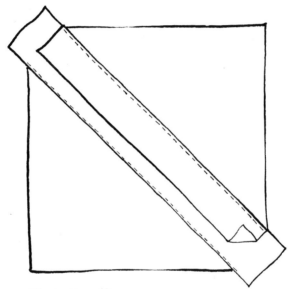

Illustration 46

8 The String Quilt [See PLATE 15, page 74.]

The String Quilt is one of the many quilts made on a muslin base in order to keep the block square. The muslin is cut to the desired block size and becomes part of the filling. Traditionally, several strips of fabric varying in width from 1 1/2″ to 3″, are sewn diagonally across a 10″ muslin square. The variation in the width of the strips makes the finished quilt more interesting than if strips of the same width were used throughout. This is a good way to use up narrow pieces of fabric left over from other sewing projects. All different kinds of fabrics may be combined—velvet, satin, wool and even ribbons. The name, String Quilt, may even refer to the use of "strings" or ribbons to create the blocks.

The strips must be long enough to cover the muslin block diagonally, but different lengths of scraps may be used since shorter and shorter strips will be needed to cover the muslin block as you approach the corners. When each block has been totally covered with strips, the blocks are joined to create various patterns. Traditionally, this block is made with many small, joined blocks creating a large quilt. I have made a couple of String Quilts by enlarging the block size so that only four blocks are needed to make a large quilt. The strips used, in this case, would be wider than those for a traditional block.

In this lesson I will explain the traditional technique for making a String Quilt, by teaching you to make an 18″ square sample composed of four blocks. I will also give instructions for making a large, "block by block" quilt from only four String blocks.

For this lesson you will need:

>   several strips of fabric from 1 1/2″ to 3″ wide
>   four 10″ muslin squares

Sewing:

Place a strip, good side up, diagonally across a 10″ muslin square. Sew down both sides of the strip, 1/4″ from each edge. (*Illustration 45.*) Continue sewing strips of random width, good side to good side, making a narrow seam each time. (*Illustration 46.*) Flip each strip over before adding the next strip. Sew the strips until the muslin block is covered. Turn the covered block over and stitch around the edge of the muslin to secure the loose ends. (*Illustration 47.*) Trim the overhanging strips to the edge of the muslin.

When all four 10″ muslin blocks are completed, place them on a smooth surface and arrange them in a design you like. Sew them together, good sides facing, allowing a 1/2″ seam.

68

Illustration 47

69

Illustration 48

Illustration 49

You may sew many blocks in this manner and join them to make a large quilt. Since each block in the quilt top is backed with muslin, you may or may not want to put a filling in this quilt. It may be heavy and warm enough with just a backing.

"Block by Block" String Quilt

The String Quilt is another quilt you can put together "block by block." Using a sewing machine, you can make a large quilt quickly.

Use an old blanket in place of muslin. Cut the blanket in quarters. Then cut squares or rectangles of backing 2″ larger than the blanket quarters. Place each piece of backing on a smooth surface, good side down, and center each blanket section over a backing. Cut several strips of fancy fabric 5″, 7″, and 9″ in width. These strips will have to be long enough to cover the diagonal length of your blanket filling. Shorter strips are used as you approach the corners of the blanket piece. Now, pin the first strip diagonally over one section of the blanket and the backing, and sew down both sides of the strip, through the filling and the backing. Continue working toward the corners, following the instructions that you used for doing the 10″ muslin squares. Although you are using wider strips and larger blocks, the technique is the same.

When you have finished sewing strips to all four squares, stitch down the loose ends, and trim the overhanging strips as you did in *Illustration 47*. Sew the blocks together with the tops facing. Your seams will be ragged on the back of your quilt and can be covered with 2″ bias tape. Bind off the edge of the quilt with bias tape. *(See Binding, page 29.)*

9 The Strip Quilt [See PLATE 16, page 75.]

The Strip Quilt is another quilt made on a muslin base. Long muslin panels, or *strips,* are covered with scraps of fabric. The *strips* are then joined to create a quilt top. If you use heavy fabrics such as velvet, corduroy, wool, or bonded knits, there is no need to line the quilt with a filling. It will be warm enough with just the top and backing quilted together. Even cotton, sewn to muslin and quilted to a backing, makes a heavy bedcover. Sometimes the seams are embellished with machine or hand-embroidery after the quilt top has been finished.

This quilt is made like the String Quilt, except that the scraps of fabric are sewn to long muslin panels horizontally, instead of diagonally. As in the String Quilt, the strips need not be of equal width, and in fact, can be wider on one side and taper toward the other. Various sized scraps may be used, and you may even want to piece a few small scraps together to make a section wide enough to go across a muslin panel.

For this lesson, *all* the sewing, including the quilting, may be done on a sewing machine. It is a very easy and quick quilt to make. You will first have to decide how large you want your quilt to be, and then decide whether you want the muslin panels to be joined vertically or horizontally. The width, length, and number of panels will vary depending on the size of the quilt. The wider the panel, the harder it is to work with. Panels 18″ to 25″ wide are easy to handle on a sewing machine. You may want to use up very small scraps by sewing them to very narrow panels. As you can see, this quilt can be varied by changing the width and number of the muslin panels, or by joining the panels either vertically or horizontally to create a quilt top.

The quilt shown in PLATE 16 measures 48″ × 54″. It was made up of three muslin panels 18″ wide and 54″ long. Each muslin panel was covered with a strip of large scraps which were sewn to each other and through the muslin panel. A strip of scraps was sewn down the center of each panel, with 2″ of muslin left bare on either side. The muslin showing after the panels had been joined was covered with border strips. I have also made Strip Quilts without borders, by covering the *entire* panel with fabric sections and then joining the panels.

In this lesson I will teach you the technique for sewing large fabric scraps down the center of a muslin panel. I will also teach you how to join three panels and add borders to cover the bare muslin. You may want to try variations of this Strip Quilt after you have understood the technique.

Cutting:

First, decide how large you want the finished quilt to be. Then, divide the width of your planned quilt in three and add 1″ to this measurement to allow for seams. Cut three muslin panels to this measured width, and as long as you want the quilt to be. (If you plan to make a very large quilt, you may want to make more panels so that the width of each will not exceed 25″.)

Sewing:

Place one muslin panel on the floor and center the first fabric piece, good side up, at the top edge of the muslin panel. Remember that 2″ of muslin will be left showing on either side of this first piece, and all others added later. Sew this first fabric piece to the panel along the top edge. Lay the panel on the floor once more and smooth out the muslin and the fabric piece. Pin the second scrap of fabric to the first with good sides facing. Sew a seam where their edges meet and through the muslin panel. Flatten the second scrap down over the muslin panel. Continue to sew large scraps

PLATE 12   Orchid Pattern Hawaiian Quilt, Lesson 6, page 51.

PLATE 13   Avacado Hawaiian Wall-Hanging, Lesson 6, page 51.

73

PLATE 14   Dresden Plate Quilt, Lesson 7, page 61.

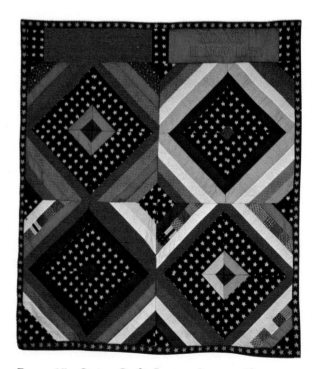

PLATE 15   String Quilt, Lesson 8, page 68.

PLATE 16   Strip Quilt, Lesson 9, page 71.

PLATE 17   Log Cabin Wall-Hanging, Lesson 10, page 82.

75

PLATE 18   Crazy Quilt Skirt, Lesson 11, page 85.

76

PLATE 19   Yo-Yo Pillows, Lesson 12, page 86.

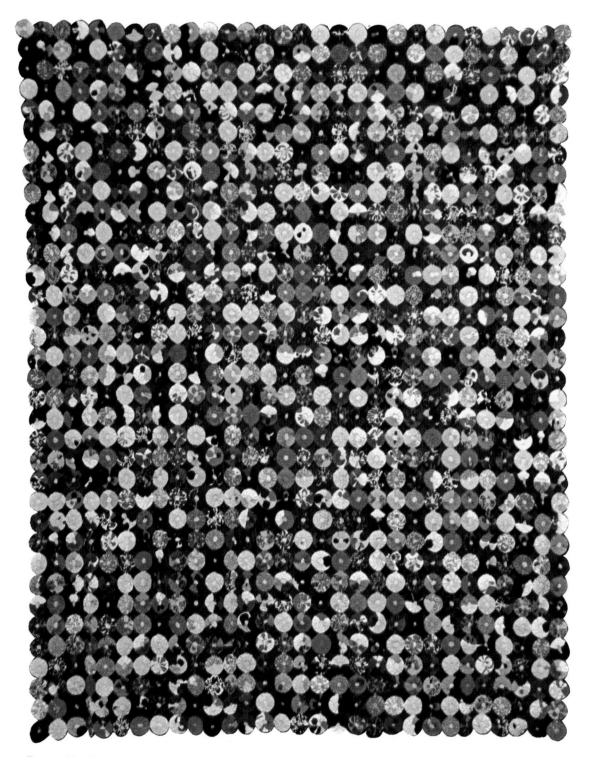

PLATE 20   Yo-Yo Spread, Lesson 12, page 86.

78

PLATE 21   The Little House Quilt, Lesson 13, page 91.

PLATE 22   Medallion Quilt, Lesson 14, page 96.

79

PLATE 23   Reverse Appliqué Quilt, Lesson 16, page 112.

80

down the center of the muslin panel in this fashion. *(Illustration 48.)*

When all three muslin panels have been covered, join them with a 1/2″ seam. Make four 6″ wide strips of joined scraps to cover the muslin showing. Iron under a 1/2″ hem on both sides of two 6″ strips to conceal the raw edges. Place these 6″ strips over the seams joining the muslin panels and sew down both sides of each strip. *(Illustration 49.)* The other two border strips are sewn to cover the muslin at the sides of the quilt top.

Quilting:

Now, cut a backing a little larger than your quilt top and place it on the floor with its good side down. Center the quilt top, good side up, over this backing. You may or may not want to put a blanket filling between the top and backing of this quilt. Pin or baste to secure the quilt top to the backing. By machine or hand, quilt all the layers together along the stitching of the 6″ strips joining the panels. *(Illustration 50.)* Bind the edge of your quilt with bias tape or a long strip of fabric. *(See Binding, page 29.)*

Illustration 50

81

10 The Log Cabin Quilt [See PLATE 17, page 75.]

Traditionally, a Log Cabin Quilt is made up of numerous eight inch muslin blocks which have a red center to represent the chimney of the cabin, and several 1 1/2" wide light and dark "logs" surrounding the center. The small blocks are then joined to create different patterns. There are old Log Cabin Quilts with distinguishing names for the patterns formed by the various combinations of blocks. *Barn Raising* is the pattern name of an entire quilt when the small blocks are arranged so that the light and dark areas create a huge bull's-eye. *Straight Furrows* is another traditional combination where the light and dark areas create diagonal stripes across a large quilt.

The Log Cabin is one of my favorite quilts because it is made up of a design within a design. Kaleidoscopic effects can be achieved by using "logs" of different tones or varied shades of one color. I have made a few Log Cabin Quilts using only four large blocks made with strips wider and much longer than the traditional "log." When using larger "logs," a muslin backing is not needed. It may even be cumbersome while sewing. The quilt in PLATE 17 was made without a muslin backing by sewing 4" wide strips together. With narrower, traditional strips, the muslin helps to keep the strips even, and you are assured of having a neat block when finished.

This lesson will teach you how to make four traditional Log Cabin blocks which can be joined to make a 15" square sample. Of course, you can always use this technique to make a regular-sized quilt.

The length of your strips is not important; you will trim each "log" to the desired length as you sew it. The width of a yardstick is approximately 1 1/2" wide and may be used as a pattern for the width of your strips. Place the yardstick on the material you have chosen and draw down both sides. Any leftover cotton scraps may be used.

For this lesson you will need:
>   several strips 1 1/2" wide of varied light fabrics
>   several strips 1 1/2" wide of varied dark fabrics
>   four 8" muslin squares
>   four 2" red fabric squares

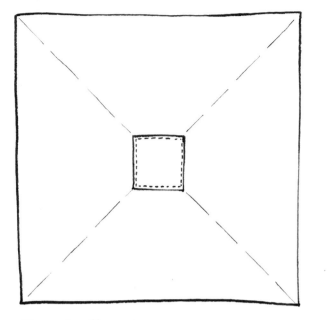

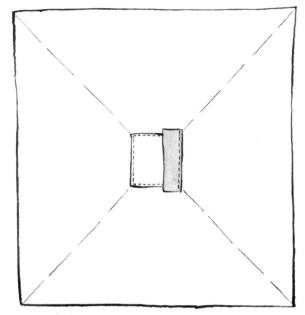

Illustration 51   *Illustration 52*

Sewing:

   To easily center the 2″ red square, fold a muslin square in half diagonally, and
then fold it in half again. Crease well with your fingers. This will give you an X in the
center of the muslin square on which to place the 2″ red square. Sew down the red
center square with the good side up 1/4″ from its edges. (*Illustration 51.*) Now, take
the first dark strip and align it along the right-hand edge of the red square, good sides
facing. Sew this strip down allowing a 1/4″ seam. (*Illustration 52.*) Trim the strip at
its ends, leaving about 1/4″ overhang on each end. Fold the strip back toward the edge
of the muslin square and press it smooth with your fingers. The good side of this first
strip will now be up. Continuing in clockwise-fashion, sew on the second dark strip.
(*Illustration 53.*) Fold back the second dark strip and sew on your first light strip.
(*Illustration 54.*) Add another light strip in the same manner. Continue clockwise,
adding two dark strips and then two light strips until you reach the edge of the muslin
square. (*Illustration 55.*) Do not worry about the unevenness in the strips farthest
from the red center. Some will hang over the muslin block and others will not quite
reach the edge. This slight unevenness will not show after the blocks have been joined.

   When the block is completed, all the strips in one triangular section of the muslin
will be light, and all the strips in the opposite triangular section will be dark. Complete all four muslin blocks in this fashion, and then sew them together to form the
design you like best.

   If you want to make a large traditional Log Cabin Quilt, simply make enough
small blocks to cover your bed. Lay all the finished blocks on the floor and arrange

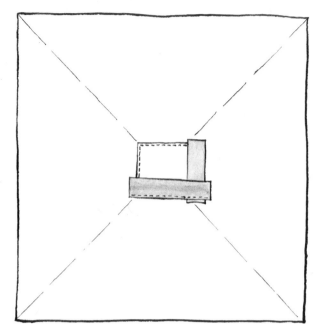

Illustration 53

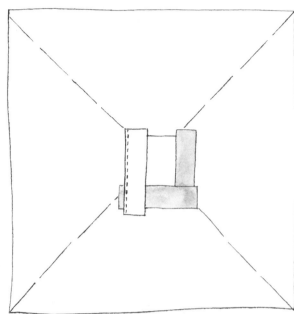

Illustration 54

Illustration 55

Illustration 56

them in a pattern you like. Sew the blocks together, one row at a time, and then sew the rows together, as you did in the Pot Holder. When the quilt top is finished you can quilt or tie it to a backing with or without a filling. Since this quilt is so busy visually, I think careful quilting stitches would be lost among all the "logs." I suggest you tie this quilt at the corners of each small block. *(See Tying, page 41.)* Bind off the edges of your finished quilt with bias tape.

Log Cabin Variation

A variation on the above method for making the Log Cabin block is to sew the first two light strips on opposite sides of the 2″ center. Then, two dark strips are sewn opposite each other, then two more light strips, etc., until the muslin square is covered with strips. *(Illustration 56.)*

11 The Crazy Quilt [See PLATE 18, page 76.]

The Crazy Quilt was a favorite of the Victorians. It was usually made of very fancy fabrics—silks, satins, velvets, velveteen or ribbon scraps—and embellished with elaborate embroidery stitches. It is another quilt made by joining covered muslin squares. If you look at an old Crazy Quilt, it may be difficult to find where the muslin squares are joined. The quilt appears to be made of many small scraps joined together helter-skelter. The skirt in PLATE 18 was made by cutting a muslin skirt pattern and covering each muslin pattern piece with velvet scraps.

In this lesson, I will teach you how to make one 12″ square Crazy block. You will be able to make a pillow, a bag or a back pack from this sample block. Or, if you wish to make a large quilt, simply make Crazy blocks until you have enough for the desired size. When made of wool or velvet, this quilt needs no filling, only a backing, and can be tied at the corners of each block. *(See Tying, page 41.)* If your quilt is made of fancy fabrics, you can bind your finished quilt with bias tape, satin, or gros-grain ribbon. *(See Binding, page 29.)*

Machine sewing is much stronger than hand-sewing, and of course, much faster. I always recommend that you use a sewing machine for any sewing which will not show on the finished block. On the other hand, if you plan to embroider this Crazy block, hand-sewing the scraps to the muslin is suitable. The embroidery stitches will reinforce your hand-sewn seams.

For this lesson you will need:
>   12″ muslin square
>   odd-shaped scraps
>   embroidery thread in several colors
>   embroidery needle

Sewing:

Place the 12″ muslin square on a flat surface and starting in a corner, sew down the first scrap, good side up, where it meets the corner of the muslin square. Use a tiny, running stitch if you are hand-sewing. *(Illustration 57.)* Build out from the corner, adding another odd-shaped piece by placing the good sides of the scraps together and sewing down *one side* of both pieces to make a seam. Sew through both scraps and through the muslin square. *(Illustration 58.)* Flip over and flatten each new piece onto the muslin square after it has been sewn. The muslin is a base which keeps the odd-shaped scraps flat and neat as you sew. Since only one side of each new scrap is attached to the block, the scrap will flop loose. You may want to pin it flat so it will not pucker or wrinkle, before adding the next scrap.

As the block becomes covered with scraps, you will run into *difficult* places where the odd-shaped pieces will not overlap neatly. You will have to appliqué these overlapping edges. *(Illustration 59.)* Appliquéing is especially useful when you have a curved edge overlapping other scraps. Pin the problem scrap flat, tuck under a small hem, and appliqué it down over the other scraps and through the muslin.

When the muslin square is completely covered with scraps, turn it over and sew around the edges to secure the loose ends. Trim the excess fabric to the edge of the muslin square. Now, you may show off your embroidery stitches, outlining each odd-shaped scrap with a different fancy stitch.

12 The Yo-Yo Quilt [See PLATE 19, page 77; PLATE 20, page 78.]

I was sewing yo-yos once while visiting friends, and Tamar, their ten-year-old daughter, wanted to learn how to make them. While we sewed, her mother noticed all the puckered circles we were making, and pulled from a closet the most beautiful yo-yo pillow I had ever seen. It was made in Spain, and the yo-yos were nickle-sized; hundreds of yo-yos made up the top of the pillow and on each yo-yo was a tiny pom-pom. Tamar said she knew how to make pom-poms on a dinner fork, and taught me the technique I will teach you in this lesson. Both the yo-yos and the pom-poms are easy to make, and perhaps you will be able to interest your children in helping you.

The Yo-Yo is a very funny quilt; even the name suggests playfulness. A quilt of yo-yos is made primarily for decoration and does not have a filling or a backing. The pillows shown in PLATE 19 are secured to a square of fabric with pom-poms, while the Yo-Yo Spread in PLATE 20 is simply rows of joined yo-yos. In this lesson I will teach you how to make an 18″ square Yo-Yo sample, pom-poms included, a good learning exercise for a regular sized Yo-Yo Quilt.

86

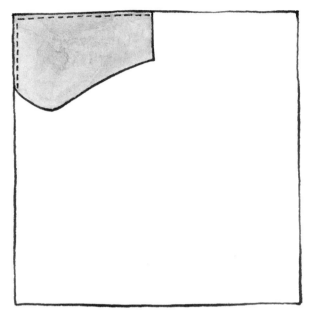

Illustration 57

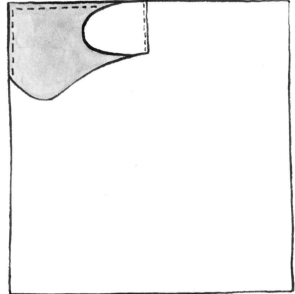

Illustration 58

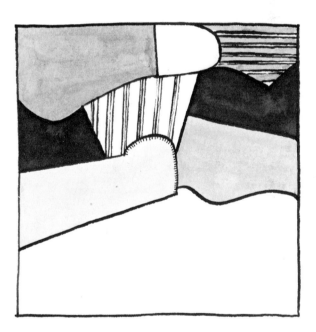

Illustration 59

87

For this lesson you will need:

> 7″ cardboard circle
> scraps of fabric
> 18″ square of solid colored fabric
> yarn for pom-poms
> a four-tined fork

Yo-Yos:

Draw around the 7″ cardboard pattern and cut sixteen fabric circles. Turn under a 1/4″ hem around each circle and sew it down with *large* stitches. Be sure to knot your thread. *(Illustration 60.)* If your stitches are too small and close together, the yo-yo will not shut tightly. Pull the thread until the circle closes and knot it. *(Illustration 61.)* Flatten the closed circle, centering the puckered hole. The top and good side of the finished yo-yo is the gathered, puckered side.

When you have made all sixteen yo-yos, join one yo-yo to another by placing the good, puckered sides together, and taking three or four whip stitches on a side. *(Illustration 62.)* Before the two yo-yos are opened, they look like a clam. Open the two joined yo-yos and add the next yo-yo in the same manner. Sew four yo-yos together in a row. Join one row to the next by placing the puckered centers of one row over the puckered centers of another row and whipping the lower edges together with three or four stitches. When all the rows are joined, the block of sixteen yo-yos will be sort of lacy, with large spaces between the puckered circles.

Now, place the 18″ square of solid colored fabric, good side up, on a flat surface, and center the block of yo-yos on it with the puckered centers up. Pin the yo-yos to this fabric.

Pom-Poms:

To make the pom-poms, insert a short length of yarn through the center space in a four-tined fork. Then take another piece of yarn and weave it in and out around the tines of the fork, packing the yarn down tightly as you weave. *(Illustration 63.)* You can weave with this second piece of yarn coming directly off its ball. Just cut it when the fork is filled with woven yarn, bring the ends of the short length of yarn up around the woven yarn and tie a tight knot in the center space of the fork. *(Illustration 64.)* The woven yarn will slide off the fork as you tie the knot. Snip the long ends and you have a pom-pom.

Make sixteen pom-poms and sew them through the center of each yo-yo and through the 18″ square of fabric. Tie a knot on the back of the fabric square. When all the pom-poms are sewn in place, sew the outside edges of the block of yo-yos to the

88

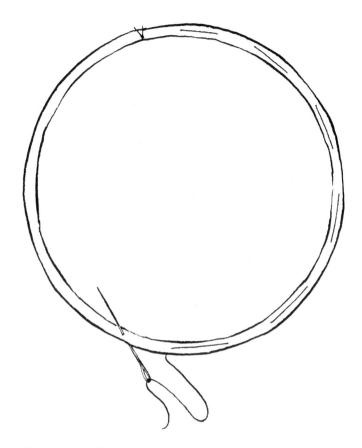

Illustration 60

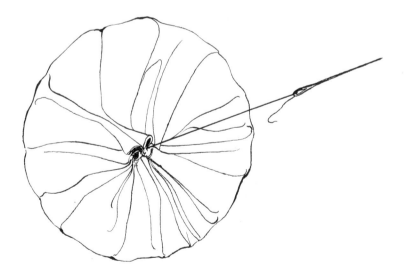

Illustration 61

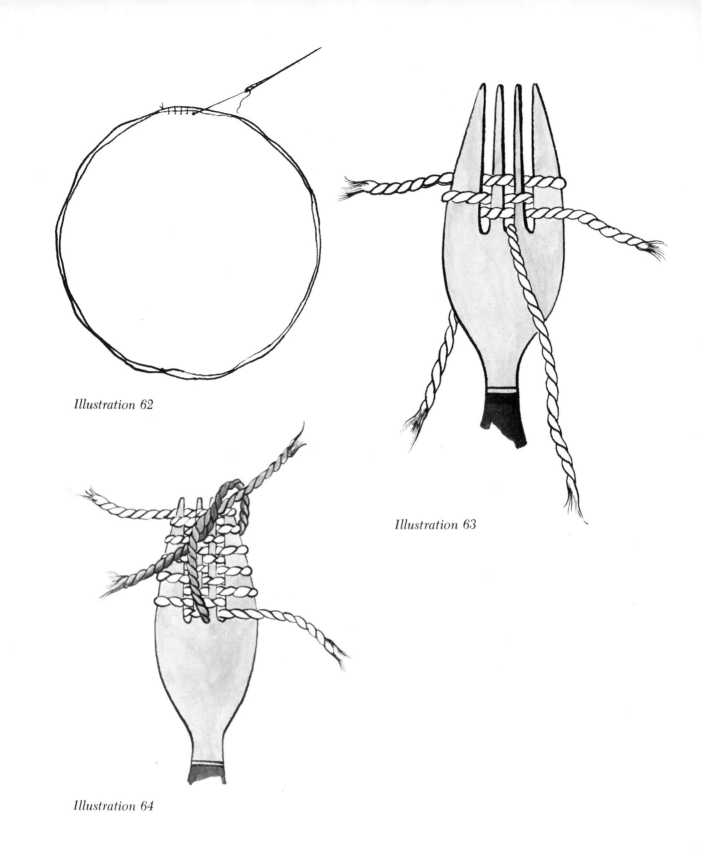

Illustration 62

Illustration 63

Illustration 64

Illustration 65

fabric square with a few small stitches. *(Illustration 65.)* The inside yo-yos are secured by the pom-poms and need not be sewn down to keep them from curling. Now you can make a pillow or a bag from this sample block.

If you wish to make a decorative spread, it need not have a backing or pom-poms. Just make enough yo-yos to cover your bed and sew them together. It is easier to sew the yo-yos together in squares of 6 × 6 yo-yos first, rather than trying to sew one long row to another long row of yo-yos. A large yo-yo spread will have hundreds of joined yo-yos. Then you can sew the yo-yo blocks together to make a quilt.

13 The Little House [See PLATE 21, page 79; PLATE 33, page 102.]

The Little House is a pieced block made up of several "house" parts. This quilt is a favorite among my students. They like to be able to recognize the houses and the variety of houses, plus repetition is very pleasing. I will teach you how to make one Little House block and the borders which surround it. The "house" is made up of sixteen joined fabric pieces which have been cut from the seven patterns in *Illustration 66*. The patterns are labeled according to how many fabric pieces you will cut

91

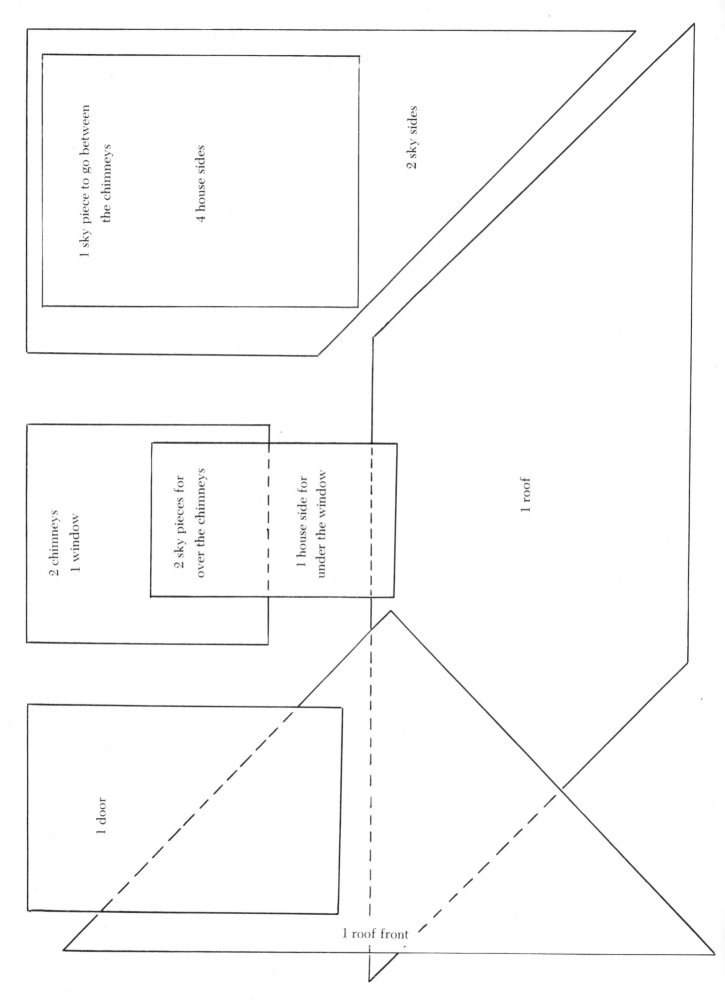

Illustration 66   The Little House

1 sky piece to go between the chimneys

4 house sides

2 sky sides

2 chimneys
1 window

2 sky pieces for over the chimneys

1 house side for under the window

1 roof

1 door

1 roof front

from each shape. I will also give instructions for putting borders between twenty Little House blocks to make a single-bed quilt top.

For one Little House block you will need to cut:
> from the same fabric:
>> 4 house sides
>> 1 house side for under the window
>> 1 roof front
>
> from varied other appropriate fabrics:
>> 1 window
>> 1 door
>> 2 chimneys
>> 2 sky pieces for over the chimneys
>> 1 sky piece to go between the chimneys
>> 1 roof
>> 2 sky sides
>> 1 strip of "grass" 3″ × 13″

Sewing:

Sew the pieces together, good sides facing, allowing 1/4″ seams. It is easiest to sew this block by completing one section, or row, at a time, and then joining each section to another, including the "grass" strip. (Illustration 67.) Do not worry if all the patches do not fit perfectly together. When so many small pieces are sewn together, they are always a little "off" and irregular around the outside edge of the finished block. Later, when your borders are added, the finished block will look crisp and neat. When you are finished joining all the sections, iron the house block on the good side, squashing the underseams flat.

Borders:

This block looks best when framed with a border. To make a border, cut two 3 1/2″ × 12″ strips of fabric and sew them to opposite sides of the block with the good sides facing the good side of the house block. (Illustration 68.) The top and bottom borders are made by sewing 3 1/2″ squares to each end of two fabric strips 3 1/2″ × 13″. Pin these borders, good sides facing the good side of the house block, and matching the seams where the end 3 1/2″ squares meet the side borders. (Illustration 69.) Sew the top and bottom borders in place. Iron the block and the borders on the good side, squashing the underseams flat. You can now quilt the finished block to a piece of flannel or old blanket for use as a pillow or a bag.

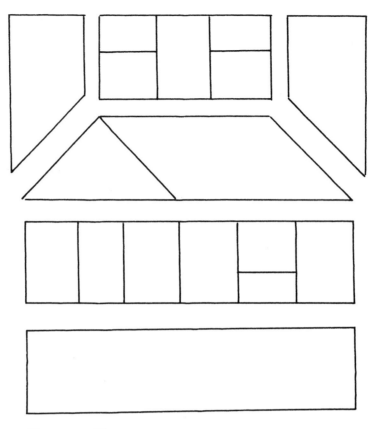

Illustration 67

Making a Single-bed Little House Quilt Top

To make a single-bed quilt like the one in PLATE 21, make twenty Little House blocks first, but *do not add borders to each individual block*. Iron all the blocks and place them on the floor in the order you want them to appear in your quilt—four in a row across the width of the quilt, and five rows long. Then, for borders, cut twenty-five strips of fabric 3 1/2″ × 12″ to make the vertical borders between all the blocks. Sew one border strip between each of the four house blocks in a row, and one strip at each end of the row. Sew these vertical borders to all five rows.

Now, make horizontal borders by cutting twenty-four fabric strips 3 1/2″ × 13″ and thirty 3 1/2″ squares. Sew end to end, four 3 1/2″ × 13″ strips, with a 3 1/2″ square separating each strip, and a 3 1/2″ square at each end of the row. You will need to make six rows in this manner for the horizontal borders which will join the rows of houses. Pin the first horizontal border along the top edge of the first row of houses, good sides facing. Carefully match the seams where the squares joining the horizontal border strip meet the seams of the vertical borders. Sew along the edge you have just pinned, allowing a 1/4″ seam.

Continue to sew a horizontal border to the top of each row of houses. When you

Illustration 68

Illustration 69

95

reach the last, and bottom, row of houses, sew a horizontal border to the top and to the bottom of it. Now, sew all the five sections together, carefully matching the seams where the 3 1/2" squares meet the vertical borders. Iron the finished quilt top, squashing all the seams flat underneath.

To make a backing for the quilt, sew lengths of fabric together along their selvages, good sides facing. You will need to join at least two pieces of fabric to get the desired width for your backing. Cut the lengths of fabric to measure a few inches longer and wider than the quilt top. You always allow a little extra fabric in the backing because some fabric is "taken up" during the quilting or tying. The excess backing fabric will be trimmed later when the quilt is bound. Iron the seams of the backing in one direction, and place it on the floor, good side down. Center an old blanket or flannel yardage over the backing. Center the quilt top over both the backing and the filling, good side up. You can either quilt the three layers together, or tie them at the corners of each block. *(See Quilting, page 27, and Tying, page 41.)* When the three layers of the quilt are secured, bind the edges with 1/2" or 1" bias tape. *(See Binding, page 29.)*

To make a double-bed quilt, your borders will have to be wider to make up the difference in width of the larger quilt. For a king-sized quilt you will need five additional house blocks to enlarge the width.

14 The Medallion Quilt [See PLATE 6, page 36; PLATE 22, page 79.]

The Medallion Quilt is easy to design and can be created as you go. The quilt top grows as you add borders and each new border can be measured and designed as you sew.

The Medallion Quilt is made up of several borders radiating out from a central design. You may choose any design or method of quilting for the center of the quilt, and build out from the medallion with plain or fancy borders. The borders can be solid strips of fabric or strips of patchwork, appliqué, trapunto, or any quilting technique that pleases you.

This quilt is mainly a lesson in borders. Once you have chosen a pattern for the central medallion, you simply measure strips of fabric and add them to the center until the quilt reaches the desired size. If you want to make a rectangular quilt, you can add extra border strips at the top and bottom. You can plan the quilt on graph paper first, or just measure the length you will need for each new border and decide the width of each strip as the quilt grows.

Illustrations 70. and *71.* will give you a general idea of how a Medallion Quilt can be put together. To begin, choose a design for the center. You may want to use

PLATE 24 Cathedral Window Quilt, Lesson 17, page 114.

PLATE 25   "Arlene" Patchwork Wall-Hanging, Lesson 18, page 116.

PLATE 26   Windmill Quilt, Lesson 18, page 116.

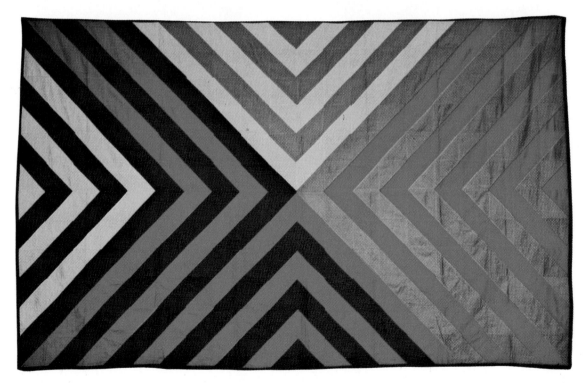

PLATE 27   Blue and Green Wall-Hanging, Lesson 18, page 116.

Plate 28   Patchwork Coat, Lesson 20, page 123

Plate 29   Belt, Lesson 20, page 123.

100

PLATE 30 "Sristi" Wall-Hanging, Lesson 20, page 121.

PLATE 31   Large Chevron Bag, Lesson 20, page 123.

PLATE 32   Small Chevron Bag, Lesson 20, page 123.

PLATE 33   Little House Bag, Lesson 20, page 123.

PLATE 34   Tobacco Pouches, Lesson 20, page 125.

PLATE 35   Place Mats, Lesson 20, page 125.

PLATE 36   Back Pack, Lesson 20, page 126.

PLATE 37   Down Quilt, Lesson 19, page 119.

Illustration 70

Illustration 71

106

one of the sample blocks you have made from another lesson. Add the first two borders to opposite sides of the central medallion. Then add the top and bottom borders. I always like to put squares of contrasting fabric at the corners where borders meet, but you can use plain border strips or miter the corners where borders meet. If you do sew squares at the ends of your border strips, be sure the seams match where the squares join the side borders. Exact measuring, including seam allowance, is necessary when cutting each border strip. When the quilt top is finished and ironed, it may be tied or quilted to accentuate the borders.

15 Trapunto

Trapunto is an Italian method of quilting which accentuates certain parts of a quilt with raised or puffed-up areas. Fancy fabric is quilted to muslin following a design drawn on the muslin. The quilting is done from the muslin side which enables you to follow the design carefully. The narrow channels created by the quilting are filled from the muslin side with yarn, and the outlined designs are stuffed with dacron filling. Linen, satin or velvet is generally used for the top layer, because these fabrics show off quilting, stuffing, and puckering better than cotton broadcloth or wool. The quilt looks much like a Roman bas-relief when finished.

Trapunto quilting is often used to embellish the center block of a Medallion quilt. You may also use this technique on fabric which has a picture or floral pattern printed on it. The pictorial fabric is also basted to muslin, but it is quilted from the front, following the outlines of the parts of the picture you wish to stuff.

This lesson will teach you to make an 18″ square trapunto sample.

For this lesson you will need:
> 18″ square of linen, satin or velvet
> 18″ square of loosely woven muslin
> tapestry needle (a dull, large-eyed needle)
> thread to match the fancy fabric
> nylon or orlon yarn for stuffing
> a handful of dacron filling
> carbon paper

Tracing the Trapunto Design:

To trace one of the designs in *Illustrations* 72 and 73 to full size, fold an 18″ square of tissue paper in quarters, open it, and place the folds on the dotted lines of the illustration. Trace the design which appears on one quarter of the paper. Then,

Illustration 72 Trapunto Pattern

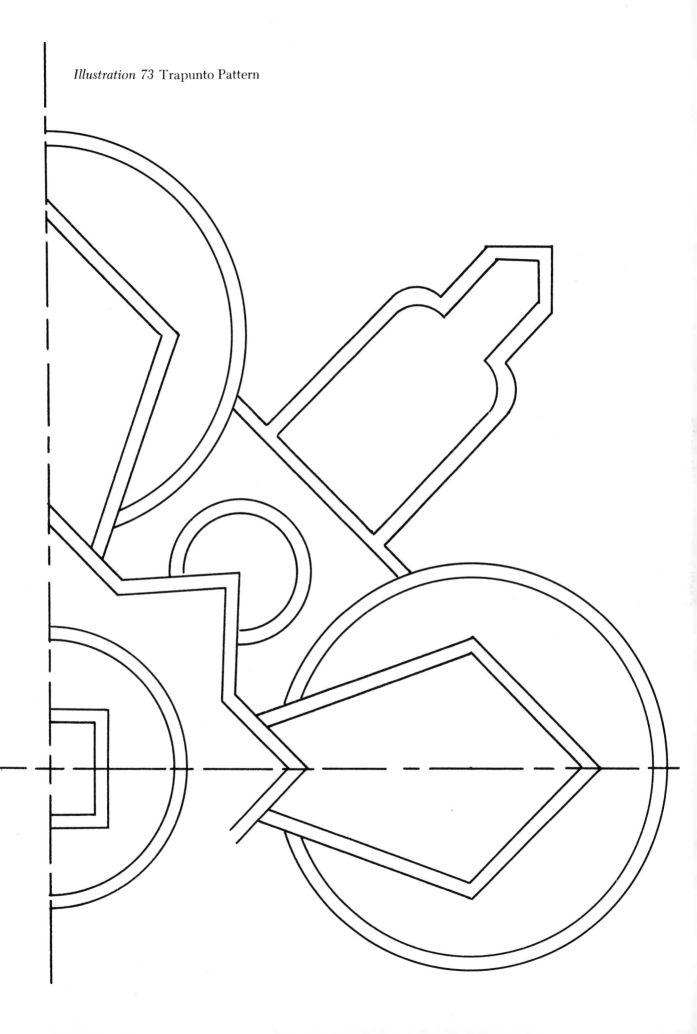

Illustration 73 Trapunto Pattern

turn the tissue paper 90°, lining the folds up on the dotted lines, and trace the design again. Continue turning the tissue paper and tracing the design until each quarter of the unfolded tissue paper has the same design. This large symmetrical design will be transferred to the muslin backing as a guide for your quilting stitches.

Transferring the Trapunto Design:

Baste the 18″ square of fancy fabric, good side up, to the muslin, around their edges. Place this square backed with muslin, fancy side down, on a clean, smooth surface. Lay carbon paper over the muslin backing and transfer the trapunto design onto the muslin.

Quilting:

The quilting is done from the muslin side, directly on the lines of the design. Use a single thread, and you may knot it. The knots will be on the muslin which becomes part of the filling if you make a quilt from this sample. Quilt both layers together directly on the lines of the design. When you have quilted the entire design, you are ready to stuff the channels and designs created by the quilting.

Stuffing:

To stuff the narrow channels, thread your tapestry needle with yarn, but DO NOT KNOT IT. Orlon or nylon yarn is best because it does not shrink. The yarn should be fat enough to completely fill the 1/8″ channel. You may double the yarn if necessary. Insert your needle through the muslin and slip it between the two layers, coming out of the muslin a needle-length away from where you started. Be very careful while stuffing that your needle does not poke through and make a hole or a run in the fancy material. Insert the needle again, through the same hole it just came out of, leaving a little loop of yarn. *(Illustration 74.)* This loop of yarn prevents the design from puckering and allows the fancy fabric, together with the muslin, to stretch and bend without tightening the yarn or breaking the quilting stitches. Simply cut the yarn and leave it hanging when you run out of yarn. DO NOT KNOT IT.

You may find that stuffing with yarn is not easy. I sometimes need to use a pair of pliers to pull the needle through. Grasp the needle with the pliers and pull it *firmly and gently* through the channel.

Stuff the other parts of the design by cutting a tiny hole in the muslin in the center of the area to be stuffed. Gently push small bits of dacron filler into the hole until it is stuffed hard. *(Illustration 75.)* Then, sew the hole closed. Your tapestry needle is a good tool for stuffing; the end with the eye may work better than the dull point. My students delight in finding or creating a better tool with which to stuff—

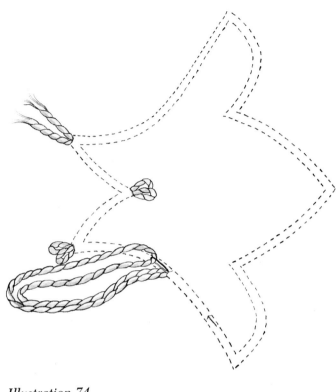

Illustration 74

Illustration 75

nut picks, crochet hooks, sculpting tools, a sawed-off and sanded toothpick, orange sticks, a tiny screwdriver, a wooden match, etc. You must be careful, if using a sharp tool, not to pierce the fancy fabric while stuffing.

16 Reverse Appliqué [See PLATE 23, page 80.]

Reverse Appliqué is a sewing technique peculiar to the Cuna Indians of Panama. They make Molas by taking several pieces of different colored cotton fabrics and basting them together along the outer edges. Then, working from the top layer down, they cut through the various layers to create the design. As the shapes are cut out, the edges of the openings are turned under and sewn to the fabric layers underneath. The top layer usually becomes the dominant color of the entire design, and less of each color is seen as you cut down through the consecutive layers. You will have to decide how you want the colors to appear, and stack them in that order, good sides up, before basting them together.

As you create your own designs, you will find that reverse appliqué is quite different from conventional appliqué. The technique demands the use of certain shapes. It is best to experiment by drawing a freehand design directly on the top layer of fabric, and seeing what develops as you cut and sew. If you try to create a pattern by substituting layers of paper for fabric, you will become frustrated trying to duplicate the paper design with fabric. And, if you try to use traditional appliqué patterns, you will discover that they are not suitable for reverse appliqué.

In this lesson I will teach you how to make an 18″ square Mola.

For this lesson you will need:

        small, sharply pointed scissors
        four 18″ squares of 100% cotton in different solid colors
        matching or contrasting thread for each color fabric

Sewing:

Baste the four layers of fabric together around the outer edges. Draw a design on the top layer and cut it out. *(Illustration 76.)* Using your needle as a tool, turn under the raw edges and appliqué them through all the other layers. Your knots will be tied on the back of the last layer. When you have finished appliquéing the first layer, draw another design on the second layer and cut it out. *(Illustration 77.)* Turn under the raw edges and appliqué them through the remaining two layers. Draw the last design on the third layer and cut it out. Appliqué the third layer. *(Illustration 78.)*

Working with more than four layers makes the finished block too heavy. If you

112

Illustration 76

Illustration 77

Illustration 78

want to add more colors to your design, cut out an area and insert a piece of fabric which is slightly larger than the opening you have made. Turn under the raw edges of the upper layer and appliqué through the inserted fabric and all the layers underneath.

17 The Cathedral Window Quilt [See PLATE 24, page 97.]

This quilt makes a heavy decorative spread. It is not stuffed; the weight and warmth come from the many folded layers and inserts. This is a difficult quilt to make because of all the intricate folding and appliqué stitching involved. This lesson will teach you how to make the baby quilt in PLATE 24.

For this lesson you will need:
                    lots of calico scraps

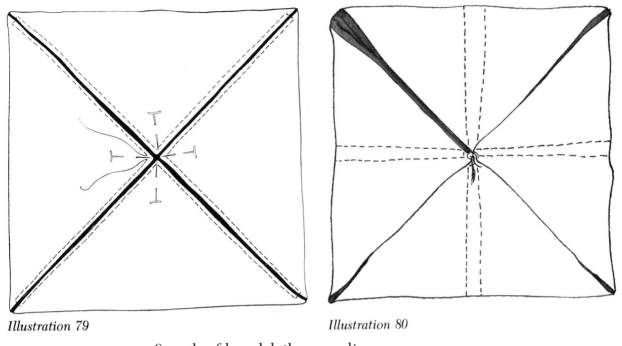

Illustration 79   Illustration 80

8 yards of broadcloth or muslin
2 spools of matching thread

Cutting, Folding, and Sewing:

Cut fifty-four 11″ squares from the broadcloth or muslin you have chosen. Iron under a 1/2″ hem on all sides of each square. Fold the corners of each square in to the center, pin, and sew by machine or hand, through all the thicknesses following along the edge of each fold. (Illustration 79.) Fold each sewn square again in the same manner as you just did, and sew the corners tightly together in the center to hold them in place. (Illustration 80.) These four corners are not sewn through the back of the folded square, only to each other. If you wanted to, you could slip your finger under the sewn corners.

Joining the Folded Squares:

Join six blocks in a row using an invisible stitch or a tiny machine seam. To stitch invisibly, place the backs of two folded squares against each other and sew them together down one side. (Illustration 81.) Place a 3″ calico square diagonally over each seam line, and roll the folded edges of the blocks up over the calico square with each fold about 1/4″ in width at its center, and tapering to practically nothing at its corners. Appliqué the calico squares in place. (Illustration 82.) Your appliqué stitches DO NOT go through to the back of the folded squares.

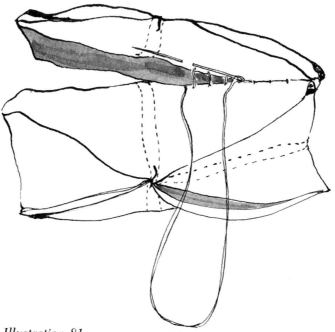

Illustration 81

Joining the Rows:

When you have appliquéd the calico squares onto two rows of joined folded squares, join the rows with an invisible stitch. *(Illustration 81.)* Fill the "windows" formed by joining the two rows with calico squares placed diagonally on the seam of each square. Work two rows at a time, and continue until the quilt is finished. The "half-windows" around the edges of the quilt should be filled with half-squares. Bind off the quilt with a 9″ border strip sewn to the back of the quilt, and folded over to the front. Hem with an appliqué stitch. *(Illustration 83.)*

18 Geometric Quilts [See PLATE 25, page 98; PLATE 26, page 99;
PLATE 27, page 99.]

You may want to design your own quilts once you have learned basic quilting techniques. Get some graph paper and colored pencils, and experiment with geometric designs composed of squares, triangles, or rectangles. When you have created

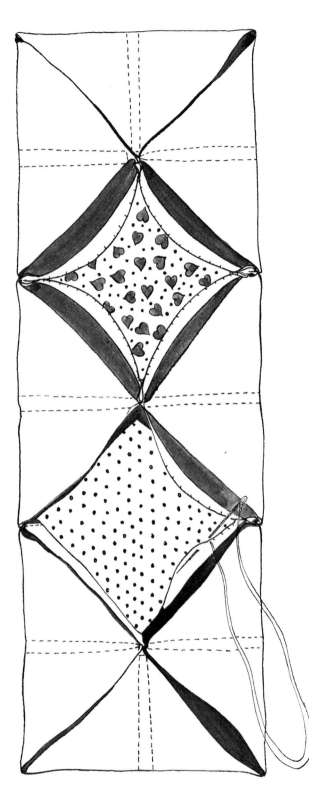

Illustration 82

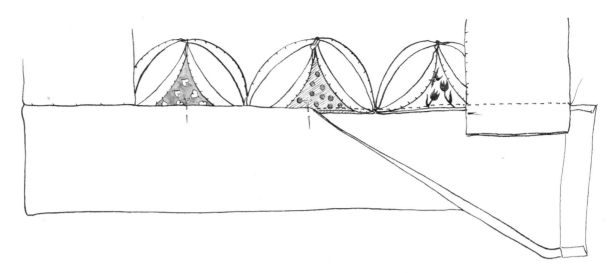

Illustration 83

a quilt pattern you like, figure out what the size of the patch—square, triangle, rectangle—used will be. Measure the width of the filling you are going to use, and divide it by the number of patches in the first row of your design. Then add 1/2″ to the determined size for seam allowance and cut a cardboard pattern. I always like to make the cardboard pattern the *exact size* of the determined patch *plus* its seam allowance. It is easier to make a quilt if all the patches in it are of the same size and shape. If your pattern calls for squares and triangles combined, either create the square patch by sewing two triangles together, or sew two triangles together and cut a cardboard pattern the exact size of the sewn triangles.

The larger the quilt, the greater the chance of making mistakes while sewing. So, it is very important that your patches are measured and cut properly at the start.

To figure the yardage needed for your quilt, count the number of patches needed of each color. Figure how many patches you will be able to cut out across the width of the fabric you have chosen. Divide that number into the total patches needed. Then, multiply the quotient by the size (in inches) of the patch. For instance, if you need 112 4″ triangles of one color and your fabric is 36″ wide, you will be able to get 16 triangles across the 36″ width. (When buying yardage, you will notice that the width is usually one or two inches less than given. 36″ material will measure 34″ to 35″ in width, etc.) For 112 4″ triangles you will need ($16\overline{)112}$ then multiply $7 \times 4″$) 28″ of 36″ wide fabric. Allow yourself about 8″ extra for error.

Many old quilt patterns are difficult to piece. You can change the combination of patches without changing the original pattern, and thus make it easier to sew. For instance, diamonds are particularly hard to sew together, but triangles are easier. So,

118

simply draft the original pattern and then figure what size triangles you will need to create the original diamond shape.

You may also want to experiment by making a quilt with a combination of quilting techniques. Perhaps you will choose to combine patchwork with appliqué, string quilting with strip quilting, or a melange of the different techniques you have learned. The varieties of quilts you can create are infinite.

19 The Down Quilt [See PLATE 37, page 104.]

The Down Quilt shown in PLATE 37 was made as a comforter for the top of a single bed. It measures 50″ × 80″. For this quilt, the instructions for cutting and sewing the quilt top and backing are very simple. Nine 6″ wide strips are sewn to form the quilt top and three 18″ wide strips form the backing. The only slight difficulty I had with this quilt was working with the down-proof lining; it feels slimy and slides around when you sew it.

The yardage given below is calculated for 36″ wide cotton broadcloth. If your fabric is wider, you will have to adjust the yardage measurements I have listed. To make this quilt you will need:

> 3 1/3 yards purple broadcloth
> 3 1/3 yards red broadcloth
> 3 1/3 yards turquoise broadcloth
> 6 2/3 yards down-proof lining
> 2 pounds down
> 2 spools heavy duty thread

Making the Quilt Top and Backing:

Cut three 6″ × 80″ strips from each color broadcloth. Sew the strips together, side by side, allowing a 1/4″ seam. Sew the three wide strips of leftover broadcloth yardage together, side by side, to make the backing of your quilt. Allow 1/4″ for seams.

Down-Proof Lining the Quilt Top and Backing:

Both the quilt top and the quilt backing must be lined with down-proof fabric so that the feathers will not work through to the outside of your quilt. You will need two large sections of down-proof lining—one which will be sewn to the quilt top and one to the backing. First, measure and piece together your down-proof lining 2″ larger than your quilt top. Lay the 54″ × 84″ lining on a smooth surface and place the quilt top, good side up, over it. Pin the two layers together along their edges and down the seams joining the strips of the quilt top. Sew them together around their outside edges and down *one side* of each seam joining the strips in the quilt top, 1/4″ from each seam. This will attach the lining to the quilt top every six inches. The down-proof material is very slippery and you will have some difficulty sewing it to the broadcloth. Sew slowly.

Line the quilt backing by sewing the down-proof lining and the quilt backing together around their outside edges and down one side of each seam, joining the 18″ wide strips of the backing. Allow 1/4″ on *one side* of each backing seam. These two layers will be attached every eighteen inches.

Attaching the Quilt Top to the Backing:

Now, on a smooth surface, pin the lined quilt top to the lined backing with the good sides facing. Sew them together around three sides allowing a 1/4″ seam. Leave one end open for stuffing, and turn the quilt inside out. Carefully smooth the edges of the quilt, pin it flat, and sew around the three attached sides, 1/4″ from the edge. Then pin the quilt flat through all the layers along the seams joining the strips in the quilt top. Sew down the unsewn side of the seams joining the strips of the quilt top. This will form 6″ wide channels which you will stuff with down.

Stuffing:

Down makes quite a mess, so stuff your quilt outdoors if possible, on a day with no wind. You may need a friend to hold the quilt up for you as you stuff it. Poke about five handfuls of down into each channel. Repeat stuffing each channel with the remaining down so that each channel will have an equal amount of down. This quilt is puffy and soft, but not over-stuffed. When you have used all the down, pin the open end of the quilt and sew it closed. This edge will be ragged. Shake the quilt well, to get rid of all the tiny feathers which have stuck to the outside.

Sew a strip of binding along the raw edge of the quilt. You can spread the down evenly in the channels by laying the finished quilt on a smooth surface and pushing the lumps through the channels. Then just pat the quilt softly all over and it will fluff up.

20 Wall-Hangings, Back Packs and Things

There are many things that can be made from the quilting techniques learned in this book. Quilted accessories are very attractive and extremely durable. In this chapter I will teach you how to make wall-hangings, bags, coats, skirts, belts, tobacco pouches, quilted masks, place mats, back packs, and pillows. Practically anything which is made of fabric can be made of quilted fabric.

120

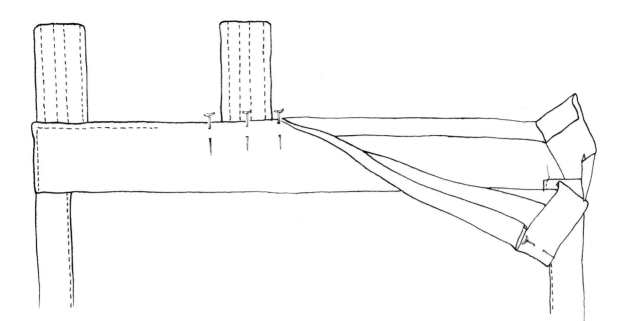

Illustration 84

Wall-Hangings [See PLATE 13, page 73; PLATE 17, page 75; PLATE 25, page 98; PLATE 27, page 99; PLATE 30, page 101.]

A banner or wall-hanging is simply a quilt with quilted loops along one side, for hanging over a pole or a curtain rod. Make a quilt the desired size, and bind off three sides by adding bias tape or strips of matching or contrasting fabric. On the fourth and top side you add two strips and iron under a hem on each strip so that you have a slot in which to insert the tabs. *(Illustration 84.)*

The tabs are made by cutting a strip of old blanket or toweling the length you need to fit loosely over the pole or rod. You can cut the filling strips as wide and as long as necessary. The fancy fabric which surrounds the filling should measure three times the width of the filling and the same length. Place the filling down the center of the fancy strip and fold the fancy strip around it, covering the filling completely. *(Illustration 85.)* Turn under a small hem and stitch it down by machine or by hand through all three layers. Continue sewing parallel lines through all three layers. *(Illustration 86.)* This makes a very strong loop for hanging.

You may make as many tabs as you feel you need. For a large quilt, the tabs should be no farther apart than 8″ and they can be spaced closer together.

When all the strips have been quilted, fold the tabs in half and insert them into

121

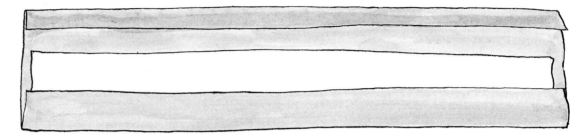

Illustration 85

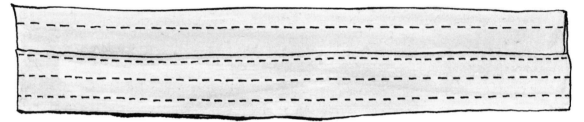

Illustration 86

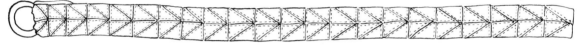

Illustration 87

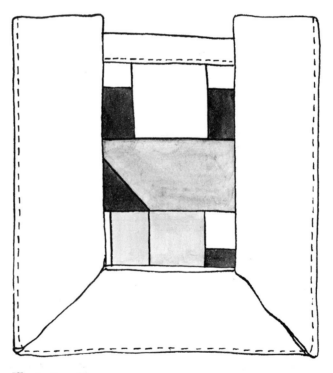

Illustration 88

the top border of your wall-hanging. Space them as you like and be careful that you measure the length as you insert each one and pin it. Sew through both layers and the tabs across the top. *(Illustration 84.)*

Belts [See PLATE 29, page 100.]

To make a quilted belt *(Illustration 87.)* simply join enough 2″ or 3″ squares to go around your waist or hips. Add about four or five extra squares so that the belt strip can be looped through a ring. When you have sewn the necessary number of squares together, cut a strip of blanket or toweling the same size. Pin the sewn squares, good side up, to the filling and quilt around the inside of each square. Next, cut a strip of fancy fabric a little longer and wider than the quilted strip. Place the good side of the quilted strip over the good side of the fancy fabric strip and sew them together along three sides. Turn the belt inside out, fold under a small hem along the open end and stitch it closed. Sew snaps on the inside of the belt so that it can loop around a ring and adjust it to your size.

Skirts, Coats and Pants [See PLATE 18, page 76; PLATE 28, page 100.]

To make anything quilted which requires a pattern, first cut your pattern pieces out of muslin or flannel, and figure the number of patchwork pieces you will need to cover each of these pattern pieces. You can then either quilt the patchwork section to the muslin, sew the pattern pieces together and line the apparel according to the pattern instructions; or you can cut fancy fabric backing for each pattern piece and quilt through all three layers at once. If you choose the second method, which is block by block, you will have to cover the raw inner seams with bias tape.

Skirts and pants usually do not need an inner lining of fancy fabric. The combination of muslin and patchwork will be sufficiently strong and warm.

If you want to appliqué the pattern pieces, cut a piece of fancy fabric a little larger than the pattern piece and appliqué through both the fancy fabric and the filling. This will insure that the appliquéd pieces, the fancy fabric, and the filling, remain smooth and do not pucker. You should baste or pin all the pieces smoothly as in any quilting technique.

You may want also to embellish skirts, coats, pants, or dresses with small sections of appliqué or patchwork—pockets, borders, collars, sleeves, etc.

Bags [See PLATES 31, 32, 33; page 102.]

I have found two simple ways to make bags. The first is to make two sides of the bag in any quilting technique and then measure the distance around three sides of the block, and make a wide quilted strip to fit it. Sew the quilted strip to the front of

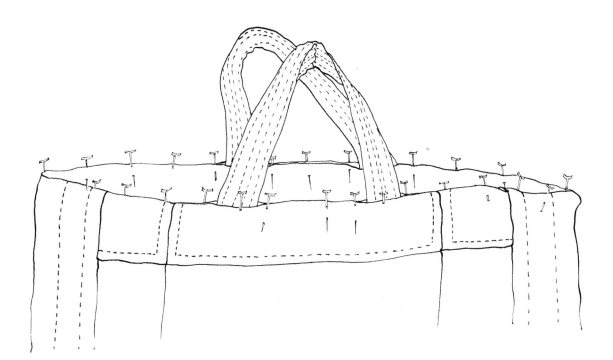

Illustration 89

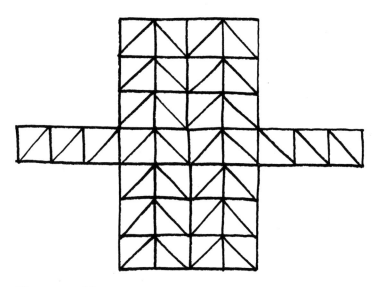

Illustration 90

124

the bag, good sides facing, allowing a 1/4″ seam. *(Illustration 88.)* Fold the quilted strip out a little, and then, in order to make a fabric "box," sew the back of the bag to the same strip, in the same manner. Turn the bag inside out. Make a fabric lining sack to fit inside the bag and attach two quilted handles *(See Tabs, Illustrations 85 and 86.)* by slipping the quilted straps between the outside of the bag and the lining sack. A small hem is ironed down along the top edge of the bag and the top edge of the lining sack. Sew around the top, securing the lining and the straps to the bag. *(Illustration 89.)*

The second method is to make the bag from one complete pattern. *(Illustration 90.)* Then sew up the sides, insert a lining sack, and finish it with quilted strap handles.

Masks

Delightful quilted masks can be made using these instructions for a bag. *(Illustrations 91 and 92.)* There are, of course, no handles to worry about; you simply sew the "face" using any quilting technique, and then quilt it to a piece of old blanket. Quilt the back of the mask to a filling also. Then make a wide quilted strip to join the "face" and the back of the mask in the same manner as you joined the sections of the bag. Make a lining sack to fit inside, and stitch the eyeholes firmly to the lining and cut them out.

Tobacco Pouches [See Plate 34, page 103.]

To make a tobacco pouch, cut a strip of fabric 7″ × 17″ and appliqué it with designs, or make a patchwork strip measuring the same size. Cut another strip of fabric 7″ × 17″ to line the pouch. Place the good side of each strip facing together, and sew a 1/4″ seam around three sides. Turn the sack inside out, iron under a 1/4″ hem on the open side, and sew a double row of stitching around the edges. Turn the bottom third of the quilted strip up and sew it down both sides to form the pouch. *(Illustration 93.)*

Place Mats [See PLATE 35, page 103.]

Place mats are just small quilts measuring approximately 12″ × 18″ for informal mats, and 14″ × 21″ for formal mats. They can be made just like the pot holder, or you can make a place mat quilt top, place it on a piece of flannel the same size, place the quilt backing over the quilt top with the good side of each facing in, and sew around three and a half sides. Turn the place mat inside out, sew the opening shut, and quilt through all three layers at once.

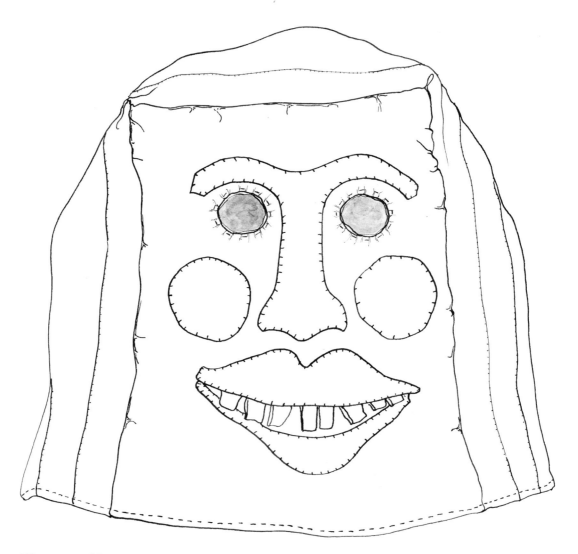

Illustration 91

Back Packs [See PLATE 36, page 104.]

Back packs are not hard to make. It just takes time to get all the various quilted pieces together. All the separate sections of the pack are quilted first and then assembled. The back and front of the pack measure 16″ × 16″ each. Make patchwork for the back and front, and quilt each patchwork section to a piece of flannel or old blanket measuring 16″ × 16″. *(Illustration 94.)* Then quilt a strip 6″ × 48″ to a piece of flannel the same size. Pin the quilted strip, good sides facing, to the front of the pack, and sew a 1/4″ seam to join them. *(See Illustration 88.)* Join the back section to the strip in the same manner. The quilted strip forming the sides and bottom of the pack will be a little longer than the front or back pieces.

126

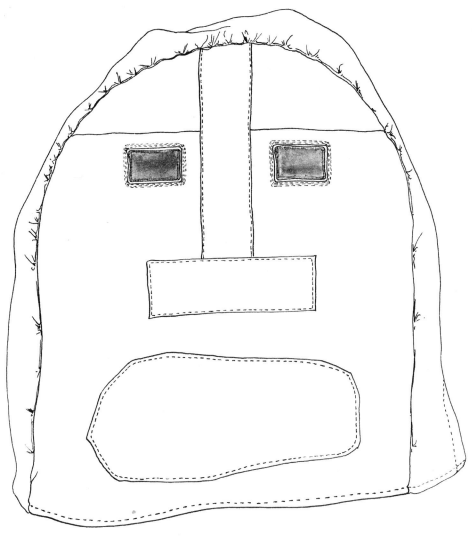

Illustration 92

The front flap measures approximately 14″ × 17″ *(Illustration 94.)* Make a patchwork section large enough to cover the dimensions of the front flap, or appliqué a design on a solid piece of fabric cut to the measurements. Cut another piece of fabric for the backing of this flap, and cut a piece of flannel or blanket the same size, for filling. Place the filling piece on a smooth surface, then the backing on top of it, good side up, and the patchwork or appliquéd section on top of the backing, with the good side down. Sew a 1/4″ seam around all the sides leaving an opening in the center of the 14″ side. Turn the flap inside out and sew the opening closed. You can then quilt through all three layers of the finished front flap.

The side flaps measure 5″ × 7″. All three layers of a side flap are sewn together in the same manner as the front flap, turned inside out, and the opening sewn shut. By

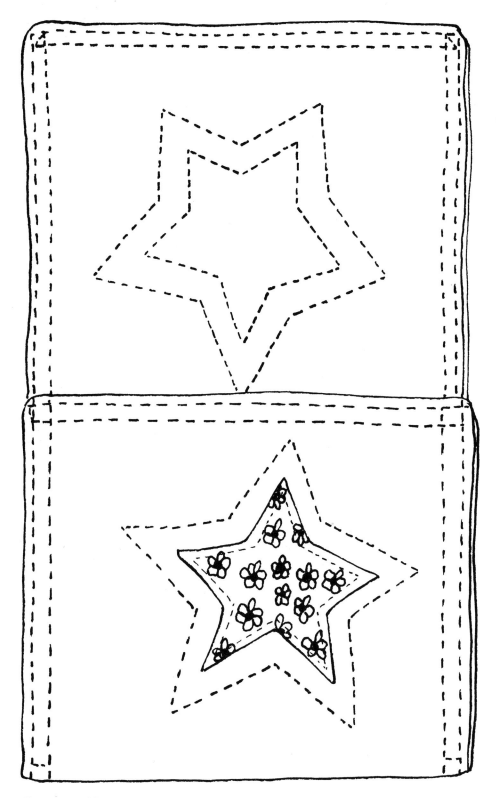

Illustration 93

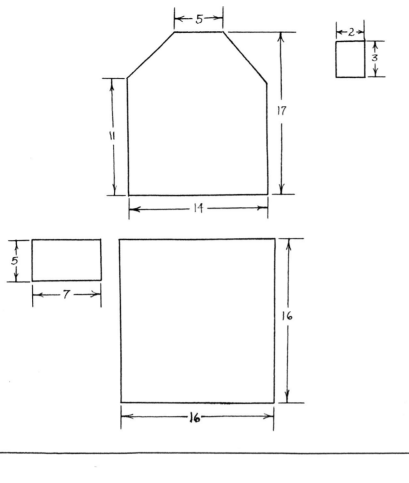

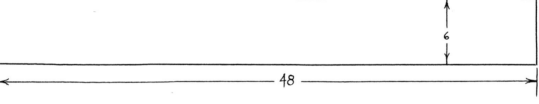

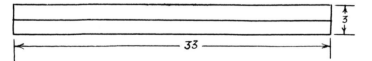

Illustration 94

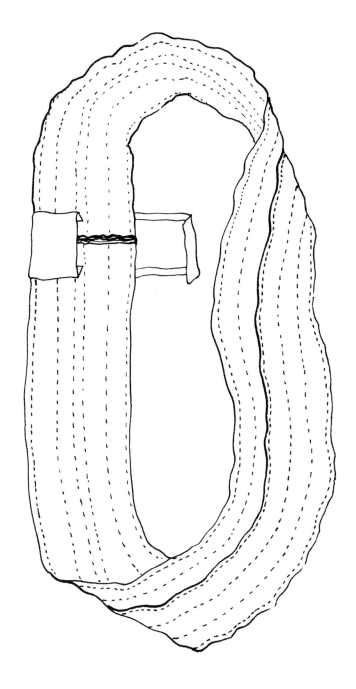

Illustration 95

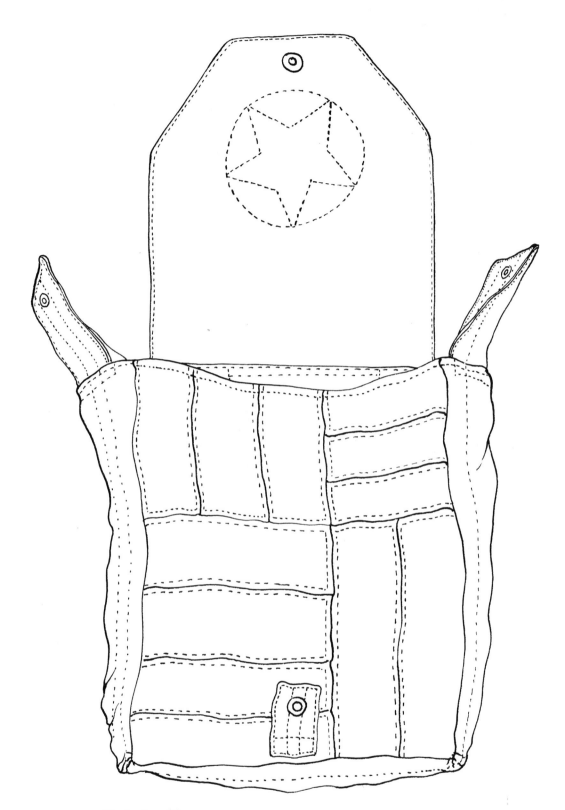

Illustration 96

131

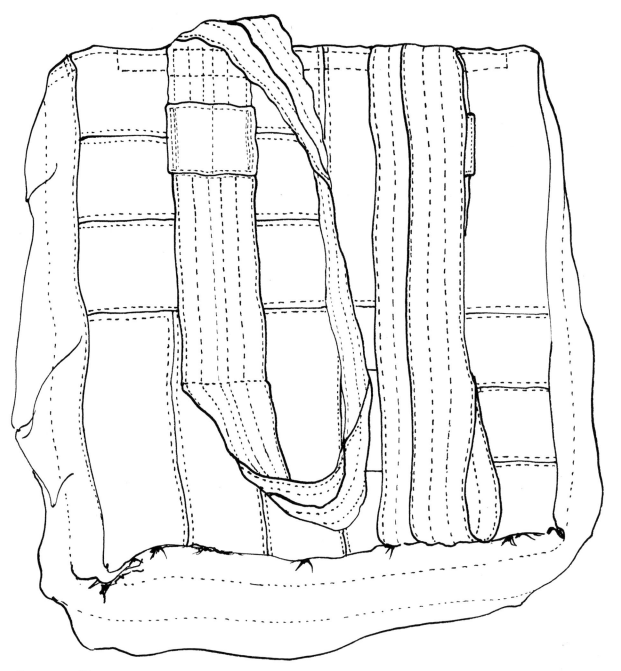

Illustration 97

132

this method of turning each flap section inside out before the quilting is done, you do not have to bind the edges of each small section. The small 2″ × 3″ front tab is made the same way.

The back straps are made by placing a 3″ × 33″ strip of flannel down the center of a fancy fabric strip 7″ × 33″. The fancy fabric is folded around the flannel strip and quilted through all three layers. Join the ends of the strap to form a belt, and cover the raw edges with a piece of fabric to match. (*Illustration 95.*)

When all the various parts of the back pack are quilted, make a lining sack which will fit inside the pack by joining two 16″ × 18″ fabric pieces to a strip 6″ × 50″. Iron under a 2″ hem at the top of the lining sack. Place the lining sack inside the pack and insert the side flaps and front flap. Pin them carefully in place. Sew around the top of the pack, securing the lining and the three flaps. (*Illustration 96.*) Sew extra stitches around the flaps to make a strong pack.

Sew the back straps to the back of the pack through the strap, the pack, and the lining. (*Illustration 97.*) To be sure that the back straps do not pull out, reinforce them with double rows of stitching. Sew the small tab to the lower center front through the pack and the lining sack, and put grommets in the center front of each flap and the tab. You can then put string or rawhide through the grommets so your pack can be tied shut when filled.

Pillows

To make a pillow, simply measure the quilted piece you have chosen for the front of your pillow, and cut a pillow back the same size. I always line the backs of my pillows with muslin to strengthen them. Also, using the muslin lining, I do not have to make a separate muslin pillow for the inside of the fancy pillow case.

To line the pillow back with muslin, cut a piece of muslin the same size as the pillow back. Place the pillow back, good side up, over the muslin piece, and sew them together around their outside edges about 1/4″ from the edge. Then, join the front of the pillow to the back by placing their good sides together and sewing around 3 1/2 sides. Turn the pillow sack inside out and stuff it with dacron or polyester filling. Invisibly stitch the opening closed. (*Illustration 27.*)

If you have quilted your way through each lesson and have reached this point, you no longer need my help. You have taught yourself how to make quilts and quilted things, and have probably learned more from your own efforts, mistakes included, than you thought you would, when you squinted to thread that first needle. You may have made several quilts by now, even designed your own, or invented new quilt-making techniques. It has been fun having you at The Great Noank Quilt Factory. If you are ever in Noank, stop by. I would love to see you, and the quilts and quilted things you have made.

Suggested Books for Design Ideas

The following books were chosen to give you design ideas for quilts and quilted things.

Abstract Painting, Michel Seuphor, Harvey N. Abrams, Inc., Publishers, New York.

African Art, Werner Schmalenbach, The Macmillan Company, New York, 1954.

African Art of the Dogon, Jean Laude, The Brooklyn Museum in association with The Viking Press, New York, 1973.

African Design, Margaret Trowell, Faber and Faber Limited, London, 1960.

African Textiles and Decorative Arts, Roy Sieber, The Museum of Modern Art, New York, 1972.

American Art Nouveau Glass, Albert Christian Revi, Thomas Nelson and Sons, Camden, New Jersey, 1968.

American Pieced Quilts, Smithsonian Institution Traveling Exhibition Service 1972–1974.

Ancient Art From New York Private Collections, Dietrich von Bothmer, The Metropolitan Museum of Art, New York, 1961.

Ancient Oaxaca: Discoveries in Mexican Archeology and History, Edited by John Paddock, Stanford University Press, Stanford, California, 1966.

"Animal Style" Art from East to West, Bunker, Chatwin, Farkas, Asia House Gallery Publication, 1970.

Art Deco of the 20's and 30's, Bevis Hillier, Studio Vista/Dutton, 1968.

Art in Posters, Fernand Mourlot, André Sauret, ed., George Brailler, New York, 1959.

Art Nouveau, Robert Schmutzler, Thames & Hudson, London, 1964.

The Art of Ancient Crete, H. Th. Bossert, Zwemmer, London, 1937.

The Arts of Egypt, Irmgard Woldering, Thames and Hudson, London, 1967.

Art of the Kwakiutl Indians and Other Northwest Coast Tribes, Audrey Hawthorn, The University of British Columbia, Vancouver, 1967.

Art Treasures of Turkey, circulated by the Smithsonian Institution, Smithsonian Publication, 1966–1968.

Assyrian Palace Reliefs, R.D. Barnett, Batchworth Press Limited, London.

Bogomil Sculpture, Olo Bihalji-Merin and Alojz Benac, Harcourt, Brace & World, Inc., New York.

Collecting Greek Antiquities, Herbert Hoffman, Clarkson N. Potter, Inc. Publisher, New York, 1971.

The Connoisseur's Guide to Oriental Carpets, E. Gans-Ruedin, Charles E. Tuttle Company: Publishers, Rutland, Vermont, 1971.

Coptic Art, Klaus Wessel, McGraw-Hill Book Company, New York, 1965.

Coptic Sculpture, John Beckwith, Alec Tiranti, London, 1963.

Costumes of the Greeks and Romans, Thomas Hope, Dover, New York.

Cut Paper Silhouettes and Stencils, Christian Rubi, Kaye & Ward, London, 1970.

Egyptian Painting, Arpag Mekhitarian, Skira.

Ellsworth Kelly: Drawings, Collages and Prints, Diane Waldman, New York Graphic Society Ltd., Greenwich, Connecticut, 1971.

Etruscan Art, A Study, Raymond Bloch, Thames & Hudson, London, 1959.

The Etruscans, Raymond Bloch, Thames & Hudson, London, 1958.

Frank Stella, William S. Rubin, The Museum of Modern Art, New York, 1970.

Gods, Thrones and Peacocks, Stuart Cary Welch, Milo Cleveland Beach, Asia House Gallery Publication, 1965.

The Great Centuries of Painting, Etruscan Painting, Massimo Pallottino, Skira Inc., New York.

Greek, Etruscan and Roman Art, George H. Chase with additions and revisions by Cornelius C. Vermeule III, Museum of Fine Arts, Boston, 1963.

A Handbook of Greek Art, Gisela M.A. Richter, The Phaidon Press, London.

Hittite Art, Maurice Vieyra, Alec Tiranti, Ltd., London, 1955.

Impressionist and Post-Impressionist Paintings from the U.S.S.R., National Gallery of Art, Washington D.C., M. Knoldler & Co., Inc., New York, 1973.

Indian Art in America, Frederick J. Dockstader, New York Graphic Society, Greenwich, Connecticut.

Jazz, Henri Matisse, R. Piper & Co., Verlag Munchen, 1957.

Josef Albers, Eugen Gomringer, George Wittenborn Inc., New York.

A King's Book of Kings, Stuart Cary Welch, The Metropolitan Museum of Art, New York, 1972.

Masterpieces of Etruscan Art, Richard Stuart Teitz, Worcester Art Museum, 1967.

Masterpieces of Persian Art, Arthur Upham Pope, The Dryden Press, New York, 1945.

Nigerian Images, William Fagg, Lund Humphries, London, 1963.

Oceanic Art, Herbert Tischner, Pantheon Books, New York, 1954.

Oriental Carpets, Michele Campana, Paul Hamlyn, London, 1969.

The Orion Book of the Sky, Jean-Claude Pecker, The Orion Press, New York, 1960.

Paul Klee and the Bauhaus, Christian Geelhaar, New York Graphic Society Ltd., Greenwich, Connecticut, 1973.

Paul Klee: The Thinking Eye, Edited by Jurg Spiller, George Wittenborn, New York, 1961.

Persia from the Origins to Alexander the Great, Roman Ghershman, Thames & Hudson, London, 1964.

Pop Art, John Rublowsky, Basic Books, Inc., New York, 1965.

Prehistoric Art, W. and B. Forman, Spring Books, London.

Robert Delaunay, F. Gilles de la Tourette, Charles Massin & Cie., Paris.

The Sculpture of Africa, Eliot Elisofon, USA Frederick A. Praeger Publishers, New York, 1958.

The Selective Eye, ed., Georges and Rosamond Bernier, Reynal & Company, New York, 1956–1957.

Sonia Delaunay, Jacques Damase, Galerie de Varenne, 1971.

Sonia Delaunay, Murilo Mendes, Il Collezionista d'Arte Contemporanea, Rome, 1970–1971.

Sonia Delaunay: Rythmes et Couleurs, Jacques Damase, Sonia Delaunay, Hermann, Paris, 1971.

Tantra Art: Its Philosophy & Physics, Ajit Mookerjee, Kumar Gallery, New York, 1966.

Tantra Asana, A Way to Self-Realization, Ajit Mookerjee, George Wittenborn, Inc., New York, 1971.
Treasures of Asia, Arab Painting, Richard Ettinghausen, The World Publishing Company, Cleveland, Ohio, 1962.
Treasures of Egyptian Art from the Cairo Museum, Edward L. Terrace and Henry G. Fischer, The Museum of Fine Arts, Boston, 1970.
The World of Art Deco, Bevis Hillier, E.P. Dutton and Co. Inc., New York, 1971.

These books were selected from the private collection of the Arthur and Elaine Cohen Library, New York, New York.